Informing the legislative debate since 1914 _____

Systemically Important or "Too Big to Fail" Financial Institutions

Marc Labonte

Specialist in Macroeconomic Policy

September 19, 2014

Congressional Research Service

7-5700

www.crs.gov

R42150

Summary

Although "too big to fail" (TBTF) has been a perennial policy issue, it was highlighted by the near-collapse of several large financial firms in 2008. Financial firms are said to be TBTF when policy makers judge that their failure would cause unacceptable disruptions to the overall financial system, and they can be TBTF because of their size or interconnectedness. In addition to fairness issues, economic theory suggests that expectations that a firm will not be allowed to fail create moral hazard—if the creditors and counterparties of a TBTF firm believe that the government will protect them from losses, they have less incentive to monitor the firm's riskiness because they are shielded from the negative consequences of those risks. If so, they could have a funding advantage compared with other banks, which some call an implicit subsidy. S.Con.Res. 8, passed by the Senate on March 22, 2013, and H.Con.Res. 25, as amended and passed by the Senate on October 16, 2013, create a non-binding budget reserve fund that allows for future legislation to address the TBTF funding advantage.

There are a number of policy approaches—some complementary, some conflicting—to coping with the TBTF problem, including providing government assistance to prevent TBTF firms from failing or systemic risk from spreading; enforcing "market discipline" to ensure that investors, creditors, and counterparties curb excessive risk-taking at TBTF firms; enhancing regulation to hold TBTF firms to stricter prudential standards than other financial firms; curbing firms' size and scope, by preventing mergers or compelling firms to divest assets, for example; minimizing spillover effects by limiting counterparty exposure; and instituting a special resolution regime for failing systemically important firms. A comprehensive policy is likely to incorporate more than one approach, as some approaches are aimed at preventing failures and some at containing fallout when a failure occurs.

Parts of the Wall Street Reform and Consumer Protection Act (Dodd-Frank Act; P.L. 111-203) address all of these policy approaches. For example, it created an enhanced prudential regulatory regime administered by the Federal Reserve for non-bank financial firms designated as "systemically important" by the Financial Stability Oversight Council (FSOC) and banks with more than $50 billion in assets. About 30 U.S. bank holding companies and a larger number of foreign banks have more than $50 billion in assets, and the FSOC has designated two insurers (AIG and Prudential) and GE Capital as systemically important. According to the insurer MetLife, FSOC has proposed to designate it as well. In addition, eight banks headquartered in the United States will be assessed capital surcharges under Basel III. H.R. 4881, ordered to be reported by the House Financial Services Committee on June 20, 2014, would place a one-year moratorium on FSOC designations. H.R. 5016, which passed the House on July 16, 2014, would not allow any funds to be used to designate a non-bank as systemically important or as posing a systemic threat to financial stability. S. 2270, as passed by the Senate, and H.R. 5461, as passed by the House, would allow regulators to exempt insurers from bank capital requirements (the "Collins Amendment" to the Dodd-Frank Act).

The Dodd-Frank Act also created a special resolution regime administered by the Federal Deposit Insurance Corporation to take into receivership failing firms that pose a threat to financial stability. This regime has not been used to date, and has some similarities to how the FDIC resolves failing banks. Statutory authority used to prevent financial firms from failing during the crisis has either expired or been narrowed by the Dodd-Frank Act.

Contents

Tables

Appendixes

Contacts

Introduction

Although "too big to fail" (TBTF) has been a perennial policy issue, it was highlighted by the near-collapse of several large financial firms in 2008. Large financial firms that failed or required extraordinary government assistance in the recent crisis included depositories (Citigroup and Washington Mutual), government-sponsored enterprises (Fannie Mae and Freddie Mac), insurance companies (AIG), and investment banks (Bear Stearns and Lehman Brothers).[1] In many of these cases, policy makers justified the use of government resources on the grounds that the firms were "systemically important" or "too big to fail." TBTF is the concept that a firm's disorderly failure would cause widespread disruptions in financial markets that could not easily be contained. While the government had no explicit policy to rescue TBTF firms, several were rescued on those grounds once the crisis struck. TBTF subsequently became one of the systemic risk issues that policy makers grappled with in the wake of the recent crisis.

Systemic risk mitigation, including eliminating the TBTF problem, was a major goal of the Dodd-Frank Wall Street Reform and Consumer Protection Act (P.L. 111-203), comprehensive financial regulatory reform enacted in 2010.[2] Different parts of this legislation jointly address the "too big to fail" problem through requirements for enhanced regulation for safety and soundness for "systemically important" (also called "systemically significant") financial institutions (SIFIs), limits on size and the types of activities a firm can engage in (including proprietary trading and hedge fund sponsorship), and the creation of a new receivership regime for resolving failing non-banks that pose systemic risk.

About 30 U.S. bank holding companies and a larger number of foreign banks will automatically be subject to enhanced regulation because they have at least $50 billion in assets. In addition, the Financial Stability Oversight Council (FSOC), a council of U.S. regulators headed by the Treasury Secretary,[3] has designated two insurers (AIG and Prudential) and one other non-bank (GE Capital) as "systemically important," and therefore subject to heightened prudential regulation.[4] According to the insurer MetLife, FSOC has proposed to designate it as well.[5] H.R. 4881, ordered to be reported by the House Financial Services Committee on June 20, 2014, would place a one-year moratorium on FSOC designations of non-banks as systemically important upon enactment. The Financial Services and General Government Appropriations Act of 2014 (H.R. 5016), which passed the House on July 16, 2014, would not allow any funds to be used to designate a non-bank as systemically important or as posing a systemic threat to financial

---

[1] For more information, see CRS Report R41073, *Government Interventions in Response to Financial Turmoil*, by Baird Webel and Marc Labonte.

[2] For an overview, see CRS Report R41350, *The Dodd-Frank Wall Street Reform and Consumer Protection Act: Background and Summary*, coordinated by Baird Webel. For more information on systemic risk provisions, see CRS Report R41384, *The Dodd-Frank Wall Street Reform and Consumer Protection Act: Systemic Risk and the Federal Reserve*, by Marc Labonte.

[3] For more information on the FSOC, see CRS Report R42083, *Financial Stability Oversight Council: A Framework to Mitigate Systemic Risk*, by Edward V. Murphy.

[4] Information on designated firms can be accessed here: http://www.treasury.gov/initiatives/fsoc/designations/Pages/default.aspx.

[5] MetLife, press release, September 4, 2014, https://www.metlife.com/about/press-room/index html?compID=140852. See also U.S. Treasury, press release, September 4, 2014, http://www.treasury.gov/press-center/press-releases/Pages/jl2621.aspx.

stability. S. 2270, which passed the Senate on June 5, 2014, would allow the regulators to exempt insurers from the "Collins Amendment" to the Dodd-Frank Act—bank capital requirements that would otherwise apply because the insurers are bank holding companies or have been designated as systemically important. Title I of H.R. 5461, which passed the House on September 16, 2014, contains the same language as S. 2270.

In addition, the Financial Stability Board, an international forum, has identified 29 banks, 8 of which are headquartered in the United States, as "globally systemically important banks" (G-SIBs) and 9 insurers as "globally systemically important insurers," 3 of which are headquartered in the United States.[6] Under the Basel III Accord, banks identified by the Financial Stability Board as systemically important are subject to higher capital standards, including a higher supplementary leverage ratio.

Ultimately, the failure of a large firm is the only test of whether the TBTF problem still exists. In the meantime, studies have found mixed evidence as to whether large financial firms can still borrow at advantageous rates compared with other firms because investors—rightly or wrongly—perceive that they enjoy TBTF status.[7] S.Con.Res. 8, passed by the Senate on March 22, 2013, and H.Con.Res. 25, as amended and passed by the Senate on October 16, 2013, create a non-binding budget reserve fund that allows for future legislation to address the TBTF funding advantage. Some critics argue that this legislation does not go far enough to solve the TBTF problem, and others argue it will have the perverse effect of exacerbating the TBTF problem. There has not yet been legislation enacted to reform Fannie Mae and Freddie Mac, which remain in government receivership.

This report discusses the economic issues raised by TBTF, broad policy options, and policy changes made by the relevant Dodd-Frank provisions. This report also discusses recent legislation addressing the TBTF issue in the 113th Congress. The report ends with an **Appendix** reviewing the historical experience with TBTF before and during the recent crisis.

Economic Issues

Context

Evidence on the size of financial firms can be viewed in absolute and relative terms—relative to other industries and within the industry (i.e., concentration). In the first quarter of 2014, there were 39 U.S. banks with more than $50 billion in assets, of which 4 had more than $1.5 trillion in assets. Ten years earlier, there was only one U.S. bank with more than $1 trillion in assets.[8]

---

[6] Financial Stability Board, "2013 Update of Global Systemically Important Banks," November 11, 2013, http://www.financialstabilityboard.org/publications/r_131111.pdf; Financial Stability Board, "Global Systemically Important Insurers and the Policy Measures That Will Apply to Them," July 18, 2013, http://www.financialstabilityboard.org/publications/r_130718.pdf. The Financial Stability Board is an international forum of which the United States is a member. A list of the U.S. firms can be found in the section below entitled "Regulating TBTF."

[7] See, for example, Government Accountability Office, *Large Bank Holding Companies – Expectations of Government Support*, GAO-14-621, July 2014.

[8] Data from National Information Center, http://www.ffiec.gov/nicpubweb/nicweb/Top50Form.aspx. This list includes any type of institution that includes a depository subsidiary. These data exaggerate changes in the relative importance (continued...)

In recent decades, the U.S. banking industry has become more concentrated, meaning that a greater percentage of total industry assets is held by large banks. Assets of the five largest bank holding companies (BHCs) totaled 52% of total BHC assets at the end of 2013.[9] According to one study, the three largest banks held 5% to 15% of total commercial banking depository assets from the 1930s until the 1990s. The share of the top three then rose until it had reached about 40% by 2008.[10] By international standards, U.S. banks are not that large, however. Relative to GDP, the combined assets of the top three U.S. banks were the lowest of any major OECD economy in 2009.[11]

The four largest BHCs each held a majority of their assets in commercial bank subsidiaries. Not all very large financial institutions are commercial banks, however. Companies with more than $100 billion in assets include insurers, broker-dealers, investment funds, specialized lenders, and government-sponsored enterprises (Fannie Mae and Freddie Mac are among the largest firms overall by assets). Over the long run, large non-banks have emerged, in part because of the growth in "shadow banking."[12] Shadow banking refers to bank-like activities, such as lending, in the non-bank financial sector.[13] According to one estimate, assets of broker-dealers grew from 3% of commercial bank assets in 1980 to nearly 30% in 2007. Over the same period, hedge fund capital increased from less than 1% of bank capital to more than 100%.[14] While non-banks have been engaging in more bank-like activities, banks have also moved into non-banking businesses. Today, a bank can incorporate as a financial holding company that has depository subsidiaries, insurance subsidiaries, and broker-dealer subsidiaries, for example.

A few large firms make up a large fraction of revenues in each major segment of the financial industry. **Table 1** shows the 4 largest and 20 largest firms' respective shares of total industry revenue for the major industry NAICS (North American Industrial Classification System) classifications. According to the latest available Census data, securities firms are the most concentrated when measured by revenue, and the industry grew more concentrated between 1997 and 2007, whether measured by the top 4 or top 20 firms. Credit intermediation, which includes banking, grew significantly more concentrated between 1997 and 2002, but became slightly less concentrated between 2002 and 2007. Insurance firms became slightly more concentrated between 1997 and 2007.

(...continued)

of large banks since they do not take into account inflation or growth in the economy.

[9] Federal Reserve Bank of Chicago, *Top Banks and Holding Companies*, period ending December 31, 2012, available at http://www.chicagofed.org/webpages/banking/financial_institution_reports/top_banks_bhcs.cfm. In addition, the top five savings and loan holding companies hold 68% of total assets and the top five state-member banks hold 47% of total assets; banks in those categories are considerably smaller in absolute terms than bank holding companies, however.

[10] Andrew Haldane and Robert May, "Systemic Risk in Banking Ecosystems," *Nature*, vol. 469, January 2011, p. 351.

[11] Organization of Economic Cooperation and Development, *Bank Competition and Financial Stability*, 2011, Figure 1.1.

[12] Many of these large institutions that focus on non-banking activities are chartered as bank holding companies or savings and loan holding companies.

[13] For more information, see CRS Report R43345, *Shadow Banking: Background and Policy Issues*, by Edward V. Murphy and Tobias Adrian, Adam Ashcraft, and Zoltan Pozsar, "Shadow Banking," Federal Reserve Bank of New York, working paper, December 31, 2009.

[14] Tobias Adrian, Christopher Burke, and James McAndrews, *The Federal Reserve's Primary Dealer Credit Facility*, Federal Reserve Bank of New York, Current Issues in Economics and Finance, vol. 15, no. 4, New York, NY, August 2009.

Table 1. Large Financial Firms' Share of Total Industry Revenue, 1997-2007

(percentage)

	Top 4 Firms			Top 20 Firms		
	1997	2002	2007	1997	2002	2007
Credit Intermediation (NAICS 522)	12.6	21.5	20.6	33.4	46.4	45.0
Securities (NAICS 523)	19.3	23.6	24.6	47.7	50.0	51.8
Insurance (NAICS 524)	13.7	12.6	14.6	37.9	36.9	40.6
Funds and Trusts (NAICS 525)	19.0	24.4	n/a	48.9	57.0	n/a

Source: U.S. Census Bureau, *Economic Census*, various years.

Notes: Data are reported by NAICS code.

It remains to be seen how concentration, as measured by the Census, was affected by the financial crisis. The financial crisis reduced the number of large financial firms, but also led to an increase in the size of the remaining large firms, through a series of mergers and acquisitions.[15]

Compared with other industries, financial firms are large in dollar terms when measured by assets and liabilities but not by measures such as revenue because of the nature of financial intermediation. For example, there are only two firms (Berkshire Hathaway and General Electric) with revenues from financial businesses—and both have substantial non-financial revenues—and no bank holding companies among the 10 largest Fortune 500 firms in 2013 when measured by revenue, but financial companies are the only Fortune 500 firms with more than $1 trillion in assets.[16] Financial firms are also not as concentrated as some other industries.[17] In layman's terms, there is no "Pepsi/Coke" dominance in the financial sector. These comparisons may help to illustrate why traditional policy tools such as antitrust have not been used against large financial firms recently and suggest that the TBTF phenomenon in finance lies in the nature of financial intermediation, which is the topic of the next section.

Economic Effects of Too Big to Fail

Contagion can be transmitted from small or large financial institutions (see the following text box), but large firms pose unique problems. Firms are likely to have more counterparty exposure to large firms, and the losses or disruptions caused by counterparty exposure when a large firm fails could be severe enough to lead to failure of third parties. Problems at large firms could also lead to "fire sales" in specific securities markets that depress market prices, thereby imposing

---

[15] According to one estimate, mergers and acquisitions during the crisis increased the assets of the four largest banks from 30% to 44% of total bank assets. Richard Fisher, "Two Areas of Present Concern," speech before the Senior Delegates' Roundtable of the Fixed Income Forum, Federal Reserve Bank of Dallas, July 23, 2009.

[16] Data can be accessed at http://money.cnn.com/magazines/fortune/fortune500/. The lack of financial firms in the top 10 by revenue does not appear to be driven by the effects of the financial crisis. For example, there were two predominantly financial firms in the top 10 by revenue in 2006.

[17] One study of the ten most concentrated industries did not include any financial firms. See Andrea Alegria *et al*, "Highly Concentrated: Companies that Dominate Their Industries," *IBISWorld*, February 2012, http://www.ibisworld.com/Common/MediaCenter/Highly%20Concentrated%20Industries.pdf.

---

losses on other holders of similar securities.[18] Some economists argue that the real problem is some firms are "too interconnected to fail." That is, it is not the sheer size of certain firms that causes contagion, but the fact that most activity in certain key market segments flows through those firms.[19] According to the International Monetary Fund (IMF), a few large firms "dominate key market segments ranging from private securitization and derivatives dealing to triparty repo and leveraged investor financing."[20] Were the interconnected firm to fail, other firms would have difficulty absorbing the failed firm's business, and there would be disruptions to the flow of credit. If problems in one market segment undermine an interconnected firm, problems can spread to the other market segments in which the firm operates.

Why Are Financial Firms Vulnerable to Instability?

Economists consider financial firms to be uniquely vulnerable to instability because a fundamental feature of financial intermediation is the use of short-term liabilities (debt or deposits) to finance long-term assets (e.g., loans). As a result, assets cannot be liquidated fast enough or at a sufficient price to fund redemptions in a panic. The use of liabilities, rather than equity, to finance most assets (referred to as "leverage") can result in losses exceeding equity, which results in insolvency, or an inability to meet obligations to all creditors in full. These features make financial intermediaries inherently vulnerable to runs—since those who redeem funds first are thought more likely to access their funds, there is an incentive for creditors to rush to redeem, whether the firm is suffering from a liquidity problem or a solvency problem. Panics can be self-fulfilling: whether or not the institution originally had financial problems, a panic can lead to its failure. Panics are also prone to contagion—the observation of a run at one institution can lead creditors to run on other institutions, because of perceived connections or similarities to the original firm.

The classic run involves depositors at banks, but the recent crisis demonstrated that other debt markets can also be susceptible to runs for banks and non-bank financial firms. Non-bank financial firms were highly reliant on short-term borrowing, through financial instruments such as repurchase agreements and commercial paper. They favor short-term borrowing because in normal conditions these short-term funds are inexpensive and readily available. The short maturity of these instruments meant that loans needed to be rolled over frequently. The proximate cause of most of these firms' failure was the inability to roll over maturing debt. When these firms experienced financial difficulties, counterparties became reluctant (or were not in a position) to transact and maintain business relationships with them. For example, major investment banks are "market-makers" (ready buyers and sellers) for securities markets; provide prime brokerage services for hedge funds; are major participants in over-the-counter markets for securities such as derivatives; play important roles in payment, clearing, and settlement activities; and so on. If counterparties in any of these areas are no longer willing to transact with the firm because of fears of a run, the firm's financial difficulties can quickly compound.

Although some policy makers have dismissed the claim that any firm could be too big to fail, many analysts believe the failure of Lehman Brothers, occurring in the context of difficulties at several large financial firms, was the proximate cause of the worsening of the crisis in September 2008.[21] One can debate whether policy actions in the months leading up to Lehman Brothers'

---

[18] An alternative perspective is that the simultaneous failure or emergency experienced by many firms during the crisis was primarily caused by a lack of diversified risk that led to many firms experiencing losses on similar investments (in this case, mortgage-related investments), as opposed to losses being caused by counterparty exposure. This perspective does not necessarily require a TBTF problem to explain the crisis. For example, see Daniel Tarullo, "Regulating Systemic Risk," speech at 2011 Credit Markets Symposium, Charlotte, North Carolina, March 31, 2011, http://www.federalreserve.gov/newsevents/speech/tarullo20110331a.htm.

[19] Hereafter, for convenience, this report will use the terms "too big to fail" and "too interconnected to fail" interchangeably.

[20] International Monetary Fund, United States—Selected Issues, July 13, 2009, p. 24.

[21] See, for example, Financial Crisis Inquiry Commission, *Final Report*, Ch. 18. http://fcic-static.law.stanford.edu/cdn_media/fcic-reports/fcic_final_report_full.pdf. For an alternative perspective on the importance of Lehman Brothers, see "Dissenting Views" in the same report.

failure made its failure more or less disruptive, but it is fair to say that it is unlikely that the panic that followed could have been avoided since the nature of the disruptions its failure caused (notably, its effect on money markets) was not widely foreseen.[22] "Bailing out" TBTF firms may not be an intended policy objective, but may become the second-best crisis containment measure when the failure of a TBTF firm is imminent to prevent fallout to the broader financial system and the economy as a whole.

While many people object to rescuing TBTF firms on moral or philosophical grounds, there are also economic reasons why having firms that are TBTF is inefficient. In general, for market forces to lead to an efficient allocation of resources, finding a good use of resources must be financially rewarded and a bad use must be financially punished. Firms generally run into financial problems when they have persistently allocated capital to inefficient uses. To save such a firm would be expected to retard efforts to shift that capital to more efficient uses, and may allow the firm to continue making more bad decisions in the future. The TBTF problem results in too much financial intermediation taking place at large firms and too little at other firms from the perspective of economic efficiency, although not necessarily from the perspective of non-economic policy rationales.[23] Because large and small financial firms do not serve exactly the same customers or operate in exactly the same lines of business, too much capital will flow to the customers and in the lines of business of large firms and too little to those of small firms in the presence of TBTF.

Preventing TBTF firms from failing is argued to be necessary for maintaining the stability of the financial system in the short run. But rescuing TBTF firms is predicted to lead to a less stable financial system in the long run because of moral hazard that weakens market discipline. Moral hazard refers to the theory that if TBTF firms expect that failure will be prevented, they have an incentive to take greater risks than they otherwise would because they are shielded from at least some negative consequences of those risks.[24] In general, riskier investments have a higher rate of return to compensate for the greater risk of failure. If TBTF firms believe that they will not be allowed to fail, then private firms capture any additional profits that result from high-risk activities, while the government bears any extreme losses. Thus, if TBTF firms believe that they will be rescued, they have an incentive to behave in a way that makes it more likely they will fail.

To see how the moral hazard problem is transmitted, it is helpful to examine who gets directly "rescued" when the government intervenes to prevent the fallout to the overall financial system and broader economy. The direct beneficiaries of a rescue will include some combination of the firm's management, owners (e.g., shareholders), creditors (including depositors), account holders,

---

[22] For more information on the events of 2008, see the **Appendix**.

[23] In the case of Fannie Mae and Freddie Mac, this was arguably the policy goal—Fannie Mae's and Freddie Mac's low-borrowing costs were seen by some as desirable insofar as it led to lower borrowing costs for homeowners. A key feature of the housing bubble was overinvestment in housing, spurred by the over-availability of mortgage credit.

[24] Evidence that larger banks are consistently riskier than smaller banks is mixed. For example, one measure of riskiness is leverage (the proportion of liabilities to equity held by a bank). One study found that large U.S. commercial banks were less leveraged than small banks on average during the past decade, but the median large bank was modestly more leveraged than the median small bank. Large banks also had more off-balance-sheet activities, which some believe made banks appear to be less risky than they turned out to be. The study also found that investment banks were much more leveraged than commercial banks, and large investment banks were more leveraged than small ones. Source: Sebnem Kalemli-Ozcan, Bent Sorensen, Sevcan Yesiltas, "Leverage Across Firms, Banks, and Countries," National Bureau of Economic Research, working paper no. 17354, August 2011. Anecdotal evidence points to a number of large banks whose risky behavior resulted in failure or rescue during the crisis, but most failing banks over the past few years were small banks.

and counterparties. Under bankruptcy, these groups would bear losses to differing degrees depending on the legal priority of their claims. Government assistance, depending on its terms, can protect some or all of these groups from losses. In some recent government rescues, management has been replaced; in others, it has not. Even if management believes that losses will lead to removal, managers may prefer excessive risk taking (with higher expected profits) because they are not personally liable for the firms' losses.[25] In some cases, shareholders have borne some losses through stock dilution, although their losses may have been smaller than they would have been in a bankruptcy. Creditors, account holders, and counterparties have generally been shielded from any losses. Thus, government rescues have not mitigated the moral hazard problem for creditors and counterparties. Because the government will only intervene in the case of extreme losses, moral hazard may manifest itself primarily in areas affected only by systemic events (referred to as "tail risk"). For example, extreme losses from counterparty risk may be ignored by counterparties to TBTF firms if they believe that government will always intervene to prevent failure; if so, costs (such as the amount of margin a counterparty will require) will be lower for TBTF firms than competitors in these markets.

Do TBTF Firms Enjoy a Funding Advantage or Implicit Subsidy?

Economic theory predicts that in the presence of moral hazard, creditors and counterparties of TBTF firms provide credit at an inefficiently low cost. Some studies have provided evidence that the funding advantage exists, although many of these studies cover time periods that end before the enactment of the Dodd-Frank Act.[26] Identifying a lower funding cost for large banks alone is not enough to prove a moral hazard effect because lower cost could also be due to other factors, such as greater liquidity or lower risk (e.g., greater diversity).[27] A GAO review of the empirical literature found that a funding advantage for large firms during the financial crisis had declined by 2011. Its own econometric analysis found evidence of a funding advantage during the crisis, but mixed evidence on the existence of a funding advantage in 2012 and 2013—indeed, more versions of their model found higher funding costs for large banks rather than the expected lower costs, holding other factors equal.[28]

Some view the decision by certain credit rating agencies to rate the largest financial firms more highly because they assume the firms would receive government support as evidence of the funding advantage, although two of the three major rating agencies have reduced the magnitude of this "ratings uplift" in recent years.[29] (It should be noted that credit ratings do not directly determine funding costs.)

---

[25] Economists refer to this as a "principal-agent" problem.

[26] Studies using empirical evidence to estimate the TBTF funding advantage are reviewed in Financial Crisis Inquiry Commission, "Governmental Rescues of 'Too Big To Fail' Financial Institutions," Preliminary Staff Report, August 2010, ch. 3, http://fcic-static.law.stanford.edu/cdn_media/fcic-reports/2010-0831-Governmental-Rescues.pdf; Randall Kroszner, "A Review of Bank Funding Cost Differentials," University of Chicago, working paper, November 2013, https://www.stern.nyu.edu/sites/default/files/assets/documents/con_044532.pdf; Thomas Hoenig, Testimony before the Committee on Financial Services, U.S. House of Representatives, June 26, 2013, Attachment 3, http://financialservices house.gov/uploadedfiles/hhrg-113-ba00-wstate-thoenig-20130626.pdf.

[27] See Goldman Sachs, "Measuring the TBTF Effect on Bond Pricing," *Global Markets Institute*, May 2013.

[28] Government Accountability Office, *Large Bank Holding Companies – Expectations of Government Support*, GAO-14-621, July 2014, p. 40-55.

[29] Government Accountability Office, *Large Bank Holding Companies – Expectations of Government Support*, GAO-14-621, July 2014, p. 24 and Financial Stability Oversight Council, *Annual Report*, 2014, p. 117.

This funding advantage is sometimes referred to as the TBTF subsidy, although a subsidy typically implies a government willingness to provide the recipient with a benefit. Note also that a subsidy typically takes the form of an explicit direct payment, financial support, or guarantee, whereas in this case, if the funding advantage exists, it would derive from the expectation of future support that has not been pledged.

Policy Options

Policy Before and During the Crisis

TBTF policy before the crisis could be described as purposeful ambiguity—policy was not explicit about what would happen in the event that large financial firms become insolvent, or which firms were considered TBTF.[30] (Certain statutory benefits conferred to Fannie Mae and Freddie Mac came closer to an explicit TBTF status, and markets treated them as such.) Conventional wisdom before the crisis was that this ambiguity would help contain the moral hazard problem—if investors and creditors did not know if a firm was TBTF, they would err on the side of caution and treat it as if it were not TBTF.[31] Problems with large firms in the recent crisis suggest that this approach was not effective.

Theoretically, moral hazard can be mitigated through prudential regulation for safety and soundness. Generally, the regulatory regime before the crisis was not based on firm size, but rather on charter type. Depository institutions were regulated for safety and soundness to minimize the costs of, and the moral hazard that results from, deposit insurance and access to the Fed's discount window. Because some non-bank financial firms did not receive analogous government protection before the crisis, there was not seen to be a moral hazard problem that justified regulating them for safety and soundness. Pre-crisis safety and soundness regulation did not explicitly address the additional moral hazard that results from TBTF, in part because TBTF firms were not explicitly identified.

Before the crisis, large financial firms were subject to Federal Reserve prudential oversight at the holding company level if they were organized as bank holding companies or financial holding companies.[32] Prudential regulation entailed supervision and examination for safety and soundness. In 1997, the Fed and the Office of the Comptroller of the Currency (OCC) set up an internal team to supervise large complex banking organizations.[33] Regulation at the holding

---

[30] Financial Crisis Inquiry Commission, "Governmental Rescues of 'Too Big To Fail' Financial Institutions," Preliminary Staff Report, August 2010, ch. 3, http://fcic-static.law.stanford.edu/cdn_media/fcic-reports/2010-0831-Governmental-Rescues.pdf.

[31] An alternative perspective is that there was no explicit TBTF policy because changes in market structure over time—namely, the emergence of large, complex banks and non-bank financial firms—did not trigger legislative changes to create a TBTF policy.

[32] Thrifts, credit unions, and banks that did not have holding company structures were not subject to prudential oversight by the Fed. In this sense, some large banks were regulated differently than some small banks before the crisis, although not all bank holding companies were large and not all thrifts were small.

[33] Since there was no explicit TBTF policy, it is speculative as to whether the Fed considered all of the banks it identified as large complex banking institutions to be TBTF. Prior to the crisis, there was not authority to set higher quantitative prudential standards for TBTF banks, although regulators do enjoy discretion in their supervision. See Federal Reserve, *Framework for Risk-Focused Supervision of Large Complex Institutions*, Handbook, August 1997, http://www.federalreserve.gov/boarddocs/srletters/1997/sr9724a1.pdf.

---

company level did not mean that all subsidiaries were regulated for safety and soundness by the Fed. Bank holding companies (BHCs) could operate non-banking subsidiaries, but banking regulators could only regulate banking subsidiaries for safety and soundness. "Firewalls" were meant to protect the depository subsidiary from losses at other types of subsidiaries. The holding company had to demonstrate that it was a source of strength for the depository subsidiary.[34] Government-sponsored enterprises, such as Fannie Mae, Freddie Mac, and the Federal Home Loan Banks, were also subject to prudential regulation by their own regulators. Prudential regulation did not prevent all large banks or the GSEs from experiencing financial difficulties during the crisis.

Some of the large firms that experienced financial difficulties in the recent crisis, however, were not bank holding companies, under Fed regulation, at that time. Types of large firms that were not BHCs included some government sponsored enterprises, insurance companies, investment banks (or broker-dealers), and hedge funds. Insurance subsidiaries were regulated for safety and soundness at the state level. Investment banks complied with an SEC net capital rule. Some large financial firms, including AIG and Lehman Brothers, were thrift holding companies supervised by the Office of Thrift Supervision before the crisis. The Office of Thrift Supervision was mainly concerned with the health of AIG's and Lehman Brothers' thrift subsidiaries, although those were a minor part of their businesses.

Some large financial firms voluntarily became BHCs during the crisis. Specifically, the five largest investment banks either merged with BHCs (Bear Stearns, Merrill Lynch), became BHCs (Goldman Sachs, Morgan Stanley), or declared bankruptcy (Lehman Brothers) in 2008.

If a bank is heading toward insolvency, the FDIC normally takes it into receivership and resolves it. Statutory requirements of least cost resolution of failing depositories by the FDIC may also help to minimize moral hazard, because bailing out firms (i.e., making creditors whole) is often more costly than shutting a firm down. But least cost resolution could be waived by the Treasury Secretary, upon the recommendation of the FDIC and Federal Reserve, if a systemic risk exception were invoked.[35] Market participants may have expected that the systemic risk exception would be invoked for large firms. The presumption before the crisis was that a failed non-bank would be subject to the standard corporate bankruptcy process; there was no standing policy of government involvement in the failure of a non-bank, with the exception of conservatorship authority for Fannie Mae and Freddie Mac.[36]

The Federal Reserve was authorized to provide liquidity to banks through collateralized loans at the discount window, with limitations for banks that are not well capitalized. In previous episodes of financial turmoil such as 1987 and 1998, the Fed's decision to flood markets with liquidity had proven sufficient to restore confidence.[37] There was no standing policy to provide liquidity to non-bank financial firms to guard against runs before the recent crisis. Such a policy did not

---

[34] For more information, see Mark Greenlee, "Historical Review of 'Umbrella Regulation' by the Board of Governors of the Federal Reserve System," Federal Reserve Bank of Cleveland, working paper 08-07, October 2008.

[35] For more information, see "Selected Historical Experiences With "Too Big To Fail"

[36] For more information on the GSEs, see CRS Report RL34657, *Financial Institution Insolvency: Federal Authority over Fannie Mae, Freddie Mac, and Depository Institutions*.

[37] As discussed above, due to the nature of financial intermediation, financial firms can never hold enough liquidity to survive a run. Nevertheless, critics have argued that the Fed's response to turmoil enabled firms to take on excessive liquidity risk. This policy is sometimes referred to as the "Greenspan put," referring to the fact that the Fed's willingness to provide liquidity in times of trouble provided firms with a hedge against liquidity risk.

prove necessary to maintain stability before the recent crisis, perhaps because there was less historical experience with non-bank runs, and perhaps because non-bank financial firms have become a more important part of the financial system over time. The Fed had broad existing emergency authority under Section 13(3) of the Federal Reserve Act to lend to non-banks, but prior to the crisis had not done so since the 1930s.

Policy during the recent crisis could be described as reactive, developing ad hoc in fits and starts in reaction to events. Ultimately, banks received federal assistance, and a lack of an explicit safety net and federal prudential regulation did not prevent some non-banks from receiving federal assistance as well. In the absence of explicit authority to rescue a TBTF firm, as the crisis unfolded, the broad standing authority was used: Section 13(3) was used to prevent the failures of Bear Stearns and AIG. Section 13(3) and the FDIC's systemic risk authority[38] was used to offer asset guarantees to Bank of America and Citigroup. These authorities were also used to create broadly based emergency programs. Other programs were created after the crisis began under authority granted by Congress in 2008. Assistance was given under the Housing and Economic Recovery Act (HERA; P.L. 110-289) to prevent Fannie Mae and Freddie Mac from becoming insolvent. In October 2008, Congress passed the Emergency Economic Stabilization Act (EESA; P.L. 110-343), creating the Troubled Asset Relief Program (TARP), which was used, among other things, to inject capital into several large financial firms.[39] The Fed and FDIC authorities are permanent; as discussed below, both authorities were modified by the Dodd-Frank Act. The HERA and EESA authority expired in 2010, although funds continued to be available after expiration under several outstanding contracts.

Policy Options and the Policy Response After the Crisis

Policy options for TBTF can be categorized as preventive (how to prevent TBTF firms from either emerging or posing systemic risk) or reactive (how to contain the fallout when a TBTF firm experiences a crisis). A comprehensive policy is likely to incorporate more than one approach because different approaches are aimed at different parts of the problem. A policy approach that would not solve the TBTF problem in isolation could be successful in conjunction with others. Some policy approaches are complementary—others could counteract each other.

Although there are costs to having large financial firms because of the moral hazard problems, these costs must be weighed against potential benefits to determine the economically optimal policy response. These benefits are discussed in the section below entitled "Limiting the Size of Financial Firms."

When considering each policy option discussed in this section, an alternative perspective to consider is that problems at large firms during the crisis—such as overleveraging, a sudden loss of liquidity, concentrated or undiversified losses, investor uncertainty caused by opacity—were not TBTF problems per se. If, in fact, they were representative of problems that firms of all sizes were experiencing, policy should directly treat these problems in a systematic and uniform way for all firms, and not just for TBTF firms, in this view. In other words, prudential regulation, a

---

[38] 12 USC 1823(c). In total, GAO reports that the FDIC's systemic risk exception was invoked five times during the crisis. See Government Accountability Office, *Federal Deposit Insurance Act:Regulators' Use of Systemic Risk Exception*, GAO-10-100, April 2010.

[39] Information on government assistance provided during the crisis can be found in CRS Report R41073, *Government Interventions in Response to Financial Turmoil*, by Baird Webel and Marc Labonte.

special resolution regime, and policies limiting spillover effects could be applied to all firms operating in a given area rather than just large firms, so arguments for and against these policy options do not apply only to their application to large firms. If the causes of systemic risk are not tied to firm size or interconnectedness, then policies based on differential treatment of TBTF firms could result in systemic risk migrating to non-TBTF firms rather than being eliminated.

End or Continue "Bailouts"?

Options

"Bailouts" are defined differently by different people. For the purposes of this report, they are defined as government assistance to a single firm to prevent it from failing (i.e., allow it to meet all ongoing obligations in full), in contrast to widely available emergency government programs to provide liquidity to solvent firms. TBTF bailouts could be delivered through assistance unique to the firm or through existing government programs on a preferential, subsidized basis.[40] They could come in the form of federal loans, insurance, guarantees, capital injections, or other firm-specific commitments.

Three broad policy approaches to government "bailouts" of failing TBTF firms are available: (1) institutionalize the availability of assistance in standing programs with standards and procedures for access enumerated beforehand; (2) offer assistance on an ad hoc basis using broad, discretionary authority, adding authority as necessary; or (3) eliminate any source of broad authority that could potentially make assistance available (often referred to as a "market discipline" policy).

The policy approach pursued before and during the crisis was essentially the second, as discussed in the previous section. The crisis left many policy makers and observers criticizing this approach as arbitrary, unfair, lacking in transparency, and too costly (although, in most cases, funds were eventually repaid in full).[41] Many economists would also credit it with eventually restoring financial stability, however, by restoring healthy and unhealthy financial firms' access to liquidity and capital.[42]

One problem with a "bailouts" approach is that one can only learn whether a firm's failure would be disruptive if it is allowed to fail. Once a firm has been rescued, there is no way of knowing how disruptive its failure would have been. As a result, policy makers may decide to err on the side of caution and rescue any firm that they believe poses risk of contagion since the short-term

---

[40] A GAO evaluation found that while the largest banks received a majority of the assistance from the Fed's broadly based emergency programs in dollar terms, they had the lowest ratio of assistance to total assets, whereas the smallest banks had the highest ratio. By contrast, the largest banks had the highest ratio of guaranteed debt to assets in the FDIC's TGLP and the highest ratio of capital to assets in TARP while participating. Government Accountability Office, *Government Support for Bank Holding Companies*, GAO-14-18, November 2013, Table 4, 5, and 6.

[41] See, for example, Financial Crisis Inquiry Commission, *Final Report,* Ch. 18, http://fcic-static.law.stanford.edu/cdn_media/fcic-reports/fcic_final_report_full.pdf; Congressional Oversight Panel, *An Overall Assessment of TARP and Financial Stability*, 112th Cong., 1st sess., March 4, 2011, S.Hrg.112-3. For an overview of government assistance during the crisis, see CRS Report R43413, *Costs of Government Interventions in Response to the Financial Crisis: A Retrospective*, by Baird Webel and Marc Labonte.

[42] An alternative perspective is that government intervention worsened the crisis by creating policy uncertainty. See, for example, John Taylor, "The Financial Crisis and the Policy Responses: An Empirical Analysis of What Went Wrong," November 2008, working paper, http://www.stanford.edu/~johntayl/FCPR.pdf.

---

costs of disruption to financial markets may be high. In this sense, the number of firms that are politically TBTF, particularly at times of market stress, may be larger than the number that are economically TBTF (i.e., pose systemic risk).

Under the market discipline approach, policy makers would pledge to provide no federal assistance to any failing firm going forward. In theory, if creditors believed that a firm would not receive government support, they would not enable firms to take what they perceived to be excessive risks, and risky actions would be priced more efficiently.[43] Unfortunately, accomplishing this goal is not as simple as proclaiming a "no bailouts" policy. If the moral hazard problem is to be avoided, market participants must be convinced that when faced with a failure that could potentially be highly damaging to the broader economy—and just how damaging cannot be fully known until after the fact—policy makers will not deviate from the stated policy and provide bailouts. But current policy makers cannot prevent future policy makers from offering assistance to a failing TBTF firm. Although it is in the long-term interest of policy makers to withhold assistance to prevent moral hazard, it is in the short-term interest of policy makers to provide assistance to prevent systemic risk. This makes it difficult to craft a "market discipline" policy that is credible to market participants.[44] Even if policy makers did intend to maintain a market discipline policy, as long as creditors disbelieved such a policy would be maintained in the event of a crisis, the moral hazard problem would remain.

Events in the crisis rewarded size and interconnectedness and arguably made any future "market discipline" policy approach less credible. As discussed in the **Appendix**, widespread financial assistance was provided in 2007-2009 to large institutions, although official policy prior to the crisis could have been construed as a "no bailouts" policy. Creditors may view the 2007-2009 policy response as the most likely outcome in future systemic risk episodes. According to the Congressional Oversight Panel, "In light of these events, it is not surprising that markets have incorporated the notion that 'too big to fail' banks are safer than their 'small enough to fail' counterparts."[45] An alternative perspective is that market participants may view public dissatisfaction with the 2007-2009 policy response as making a repeat unlikely.

Although it is impossible to prevent future policy makers from making statutory changes to current policy, current policy makers can make it more difficult for future policy makers to "bail out" firms by repealing or limiting the existing standing authority that policy makers used to provide assistance in the crisis. Enacting new authority is likely to be a higher hurdle than invoking existing authority. Examples of standing authority include the Fed's 13(3) emergency authority and the FDIC's systemic risk exception to least cost resolution. The advantage to maintaining broad discretionary emergency authority is that it allows policy makers to react quickly to unforeseen contingencies, and the authority may be used for other purposes than bailouts, as defined in this report. If assistance became necessary in a fast-moving crisis, new authority might take too long to enact. By then, the damage to the economy could be worse. In other words, eliminating broad authority could still result in a TBTF rescue, but after more financial disruption had occurred. TARP is an example of authority that was enacted relatively

---

[43] As will be discussed in the section below entitled "Resolving a Large, Interconnected Failing Firm," the failure could be resolved by the bankruptcy process or a special receivership regime, similar to how banks are resolved. If the latter is used, then issues arise as to what government support becomes available to creditors through the receiver.

[44] Economists refer to this as a "time inconsistency" problem. See Gary Stern and Ron Feldman, *Too Big to Fail*, Brookings Institute Press, Washington, D.C., 2004, ch. 2.

[45] Congressional Oversight Panel, *March Oversight Report*, March 16, 2011, p. 153, http://frwebgate.access.gpo.gov/cgi-bin/getdoc.cgi?dbname=112_senate_hearings&docid=f:64832.pdf.

quickly during a crisis; nevertheless, its enactment took weeks, whereas contagion can spread in days.

If one believes that assistance is inevitable because of short-term incentives, there are two advantages to institutionalizing the terms of assistance. First, making the terms and conditions explicit reduces the likelihood that assistance could be provided arbitrarily or on the basis of favoritism, and provides an opportunity to create a funding mechanism so that funding is not shifted to the taxpayer. Second, an explicit policy avoids policy uncertainty, which can heighten systemic risk. Arguably, lack of explicit policy added to the panic after Lehman Brothers failed, because market participants may have incorrectly based decisions on the expectation that Lehman Brothers would receive the same type of government assistance that Bear Stearns received.[46] A drawback is that setting forth standards for coping with problems at large firms before the fact could make the moral hazard problem worse by leaving no ambiguity about which firms will receive assistance.

A related approach would be to allow TBTF firms to fail, but stop contagion by creating standing credit facilities ahead of time to aid solvent counterparties. This would reduce moral hazard on the firm's part (because its managers would have a greater incentive to avoid failure), but would not eliminate it because counterparties would have less reason to monitor the firm's riskiness. An example of this approach is the decision to let Lehman Brothers fail, then subsequently offer a blanket guarantee for money market mutual funds (MMFs) to prevent a run triggered by one such fund's financial difficulties related to its holdings of Lehman debt.[47] As the MMF example illustrates, sometimes this approach could require assistance to be extended much more broadly than to just direct counterparties. Further, if standing facilities are too easily accessed, they could crowd out private inter-firm lending.

The optimal approach to bailouts from an economic perspective is arguably the one that is least costly to the economy in the short and long run. The cost of TBTF to the economy includes the direct expenditures by the government and the costs of a less stable financial system due to moral hazard. It can be argued that a failure to bail out TBTF firms would make the system less stable, because it would potentially allow systemic risk to spread. Alternatively, if bailouts increase moral hazard, it can be argued that greater moral hazard causes the system to be less stable by encouraging TBTF firms to act less prudently. However, even without moral hazard, firms would sometimes fail, as finance is inherently risky.

The 2008 experience lacks a counterfactual to definitively answer the question of which approach is least costly in the short run. The crisis worsened after Lehman Brothers was allowed to fail and ended after TARP and other broadly based emergency programs were created. Ad hoc rescues of failing TBTF firms had not succeeded in stabilizing financial markets to that point, but it is unknown whether financial conditions would have eventually normalized had that ad hoc policy been pursued consistently and continually. There is also no counterfactual as to what would have happened if there had been a consistent policy of allowing firms to fail in the crisis dating back to Bear Stearns, but the outcome that policy makers believed would occur if Bear Stearns had not been rescued is similar to events following the Lehman Brothers bankruptcy.

---

[46] See, for example, John Taylor, "The Financial Crisis and the Policy Responses: An Empirical Analysis of What Went Wrong," November 2008, working paper, http://www.stanford.edu/~johntayl/FCPR.pdf.

[47] For more information, see the **Appendix**.

During the crisis, it appeared that the ultimate cost to the government of TBTF "bailouts" could run into the hundreds of billions, collectively.[48] In hindsight, all of the special assistance to large financial firms (Bear Stearns, the GSEs, Ally Financial, Chrysler Financial, AIG, Citigroup, and Bank of America), as well as the broadly based emergency programs that large and small financial firms accessed, turned out to be cash-flow positive for the government (i.e., income and principal repayments exceeded outlays).[49] Cash-flow measures, however, do not reflect the economic cost of assistance, which would factor in the rate of return a private investor would have required to make a similar investment, incorporating risk and the time value of money. On an economic basis, CBO has estimated that special assistance through TARP to Citigroup, Bank of America and broadly based programs have generated positive profits for the government, while the TARP assistance to AIG and the auto finance firms was subsidized.[50] Although there were ultimately no net losses in these cases, these government interventions exposed the government to large potential losses.

Estimates of the cost to the government of "bailouts" do not include the broader costs of a systemic disruption to the economy, which would have feedback effects on the federal budget. In this sense, the question of whether it is more costly to bail out TBTF firms or allow them to fail cannot be definitively settled. Arguably, it was the government's interventions following Lehman Brothers' collapse that ultimately ended the panic, as measured by standard measures of financial stress such as the spread between Treasury rates and the London Inter-bank Offering Rate (LIBOR), which did not begin to fall until legislation creating TARP was enacted.[51]

Policy Response

Maintaining broad discretionary authority, but attempting to limit its scope to prevent bailing out insolvent firms could be seen as the approach taken by Title XI of the Dodd-Frank Act. It limits the Fed to providing emergency assistance only through widely available facilities, requires the Fed to issue rules and regulations on how such assistance will be provided, and prohibits the Fed from lending to failing firms. It also created new statutory authority for the FDIC to set up emergency liquidity programs in the future with restrictions and limitations, including that the recipient must be solvent, rather than allowing the FDIC to again rely on an open-ended systemic risk exception. Critics would argue that emergency authority remains broad enough under the Dodd-Frank Act that regulators would be likely to use it to save TBTF firms in the future. The Dodd-Frank Act did not institutionalize a broadly based capital injection program similar to TARP's Capital Purchase Program, which expired in 2010.

---

[48] For example, CBO expected TARP alone to have a subsidy cost of $190 billion in January 2009. See Congressional Budget Office, *The Budget and Economic Outlook*, January 2009, p. 25.

[49] CRS Report R43413, *Costs of Government Interventions in Response to the Financial Crisis: A Retrospective*, by Baird Webel and Marc Labonte.

[50] Congressional Budget Office, *Report on the Troubled Asset Relief Program*, April 2014. There is no recent estimate of the economic costs for programs outside of TARP. Economic gains on assistance to AIG outside of TARP partly or wholly offset economic costs to AIG through TARP.

[51] An alternative perspective is that government intervention worsened the crisis by creating policy uncertainty. See, for example, John Taylor, "The Financial Crisis and the Policy Responses: An Empirical Analysis of What Went Wrong," November 2008, working paper, http://www.stanford.edu/~johntayl/FCPR.pdf.

Limiting the Size of Financial Firms

Options

One approach to eliminating TBTF is to alter the characteristics of firms that make them TBTF. If TBTF is primarily a function of size, policy makers could require TBTF firms to sell businesses, divest assets, or break up to the point that they are no longer TBTF. Size can be measured in different ways, and regulators would likely need to use discretion to weigh a number of measures.[52] It is also not obvious at what size a firm becomes a source of systemic risk—should the line be drawn at, say, $1 trillion, $100 billion, or $50 billion of assets?—and could not be confirmed until firms failed. A firm could be TBTF because of its overall size or because of its size or importance in a particular segment of the financial market, suggesting that overall size alone may not be a sufficient determinant of systemic importance. It is also possible that if all institutions were smaller because of a size cap, the largest institutions would still be systemically important, even though their size would not be large by today's standards. A parallel might be the decision to rescue Continental Illinois in 1984—it was the seventh-largest bank, but had assets of only $45 billion at its peak, as geographic restrictions meant that the average size of all banks was smaller.[53]

The benefits of reducing the size of firms are that, if successful, it could eliminate the moral hazard and the need for future "bailouts" stemming from TBTF. Other potential costs and benefits are more ambiguous. Size restrictions may raise the cost or reduce the quality of financial products currently provided by TBTF firms to consumers and investors; whether this is good or bad from an economic perspective depends on the cause. If low costs currently stem primarily from the TBTF "subsidy," then economic efficiency would improve if large firms are eliminated even if costs rose as a result.[54] Alternatively, if low costs currently stem primarily from economies of scale, then economic efficiency would be reduced by size restrictions.[55] Beyond cost, large firms may make markets more liquid and enhance customer convenience (such as a nationwide physical presence). Large non-financial firms may also have financial needs (such as the underwriting of securities) that would overwhelm small financial firms.[56] Similarly, if the success of the largest firms comes primarily through their ability to innovate and provide more sophisticated or superior products, then size restrictions could reduce economic efficiency.[57]

---

[52] One variation on this approach would be to cap borrowing, so that a firm would face no size limit when financing its activities through capital, but in effect could not grow past a specified threshold through the use of leverage.

[53] Federal Deposit Insurance Corporation, "Continental Illinois and 'Too Big to Fail'," *History of the Eighties*, Ch. 7, http://www.fdic.gov/bank/historical/history/235_258.pdf. For more information, see the section below on Continental Illinois in the **Appendix**.

[54] See, for example, Anat R. Admati *et al*, "Fallacies, Irrelevant Facts, and Myths in the Discussion of Capital Regulation: Why Bank Equity is Not Expensive," working paper, March 23, 2011, https://gsbapps.stanford.edu/researchpapers/library/RP2065R1&86.pdf.

[55] The evidence on the existence of economies of scale is reviewed in Inci Otker-Robe et al, "The Too-Important-to Fail Conundrum," International Monetary Fund, *Staff Discussion Note SGN/11/12*, May 2011, available at http://www.imf.org/external/pubs/ft/sdn/2011/sdn1112.pdf. See also David Wheelock and Paul Wilson, "Do Large Banks Have Lower Costs? New Estimates of Returns to Scale for U.S. Banks," Federal Reserve Bank of St. Louis, Working Paper 2009-054E, May 2011, http://research.stlouisfed.org/wp/2009/2009-054.pdf.

[56] According to Hamilton Place Strategies, the largest syndicated loan in 2012 involved underwriting by the four largest U.S. banks and two foreign banks. See Hamilton Place Strategies, "Banking on Our Future," *HPSinsight*, February 2013.

[57] These benefits are also discussed in Hamilton Place Strategies, "Banking on Our Future," *HPSinsight*, February 2013.

Alternatively, if success of large firms comes primarily through the ability to extract monopoly rents, size restrictions could improve economic efficiency.[58] While reducing size should reduce systemic risk, there is mixed evidence on whether large firms are more or less likely to fail than small firms.[59] They could be less likely to fail because of greater diversification or more sophisticated risk management. Canada's unique experience in avoiding the recent financial crisis is attributed by some to its highly concentrated banking system.[60]

Unless rules to limit the size of financial firms are global, size restrictions could place U.S. firms at a disadvantage at home and abroad in their competition with foreign financial firms. (Some types of financial activities can be performed abroad more easily than others, so the relevance of this factor depends on the activity in question.) If business were to shift to large foreign firms, the overall level of systemic risk in the financial system (which already involves large international capital flows) may not decline, or could even increase if prudential regulation in the foreign firm's home country were inferior to U.S. regulation.

An alternative to restricting size would be to penalize size through a tax or assessment on assets or liabilities above a stated threshold. In theory, the tax could be set at the rate that would neutralize any funding advantage that a bank enjoys because of its TBTF status. Given that it is uncertain at what size a financial firm becomes TBTF, a tax could be viewed as less harmful than a cap if set at the wrong threshold and perhaps more easily adjusted over time. Other policy options that raise funding costs for large firms, such as higher capital requirements, can be viewed as having a similar effect to a tax.[61]

If policy makers decided to reduce the size of firms, a phase-in or transition period might be desirable to avoid significant short-term disruptions to the overall financial system. Likewise, when designing a policy that applies only to firms above a size threshold, one consideration is whether to make the threshold graduated to avoid cliff effects. Otherwise, firms might take actions to remain just below the threshold.

Policy Response

Section 121 of the Dodd-Frank Act allows the Federal Reserve to prevent mergers and acquisitions, restrict the products a firm is allowed to offer, terminate activities, and sell assets if the Federal Reserve and at least two-thirds of the Financial Stability Oversight Council believes that a firm that has more than $50 billion in assets poses a "grave threat to the financial stability of the United States." It does not allow the Fed to undertake these actions simply because a firm is large. Before the crisis, a BHC was limited to holding no more than 10% of national deposits and 30% of any state's deposits.

---

[58] Financial Stability Oversight Council, *Study and Recommendations Regarding Concentration Limits on Large Financial Companies*, January 2011, http://www.treasury.gov/initiatives/Documents/Study%20on%20Concentration%20Limits%20on%20Large%20Firms%2001-17-11.pdf.

[59] See Thorsten Beck, "Bank Competition and Financial Stability, Friends or Foes?," in *Competition in the Financial Sector*, Bank Indonesia and Banco de Mexico, 2008; Antonio Ruiz-Porras, "Banking competition and financial fragility: Evidence from panel-data, *Estudios Economicos*, vol. 23, no. 1, 2008.

[60] See Renee Haltom, "Why Was Canada Exempt From the Financial Crisis?, *Economic* Focus, Fourth Quarter, 2013, p. 22.

[61] See Jeremy Stein, "Regulating Large Financial Institutions," speech at the International Monetary Fund, April 17, 2013.

Section 622 of the Dodd-Frank Act prevents mergers or consolidations that would result in a firm with more than 10% of total liabilities of certain financial firms or, in the case of a bank, 10% of the total amount of deposits of insured depository institutions in the United States. This limit can be waived in the case of the acquisition of a failing firm. The limit does not prevent firms from increasing their market share "organically." The FSOC has determined that Section 622 will limit the acquisitions of only the four largest bank holding companies at this time.[62] A proposed rule implementing the limit was released in May 2014.[63]

The Dodd-Frank Act allowed fees to be assessed on banks with more than $50 billion in assets and non-banks designated as systemically important. The fees were intended to finance the costs of supervision and resolution, as well as the budget of the Office of Financial Research, as opposed to being punitive, however.

Limiting the Scope of Financial Firms

Options

The activities in which bank subsidiaries may engage are restricted by statute, but bank holding companies may own non-bank subsidiaries.[64] The subsidiaries of, and off-balance sheet entities associated with, the largest BHCs are active participants, to varying degrees, in multiple lines of business outside of traditional bank lending, including asset-backed securitization, trust services, insurance, money market mutual funds, and broker-dealers.[65] A large firm's presence throughout the financial system is one source of its "interconnectedness."

Imposing a size restriction on firms is relatively straightforward—it requires establishing a measure of size, identifying the threshold size that makes a firm TBTF, and preventing firms from exceeding that threshold. Altering firms so that they are not too interconnected to fail is more complicated because there is less consensus on what characteristics make a firm "too interconnected."[66] If interconnectedness is taken to mean that the firm is an important participant in several different segments of financial markets, then policy makers could take what has popularly been described as the "reinstate Glass-Steagall" approach.[67] The essence of this proposal is to prevent a single financial holding company from operating in multiple lines of

---

[62] Financial Stability Oversight Council, *Study and Recommendations Regarding Concentration Limits on Large Financial Companies*, January 2011, p. 8, http://www.treasury.gov/initiatives/Documents/Study%20on%20Concentration%20Limits%20on%20Large%20Firms%2001-17-11.pdf.

[63] It can be accessed at http://federalreserve.gov/newsevents/press/bcreg/20140508a.htm.

[64] For more information, see the **Appendix**.

[65] Tobias Adrian and Adam Ashcraft, "Shadow Banking: A Review of the Literature," Federal Reserve Bank of New York, Staff Report no. 580, October 2012.

[66] The Financial Stability Oversight Council has grappled with coming up with developing metrics for these concepts in its rulemaking (12 CFR Part 1310, RIN 4030-AA00). Different perspectives on defining the concepts can be found in the public comments to the rulemaking. See also International Monetary Fund, Bank for International Settlements, Financial Stability Board, *Guidance to Assess the Systemic Importance of Financial Institutions, Markets and Instruments*, report, October 2009, available at http://www.imf.org/external/np/g20/pdf/100109.pdf.

[67] Reinstating the Glass-Steagall Act in its entirety would involve many other policy areas as well that have changed significantly over time. Proponents of reinstating Glass-Steagall are usually understood to be focused on four key provisions. For more information, see CRS Report R41181, *Permissible Securities Activities of Commercial Banks Under the Glass-Steagall Act (GSA) and the Gramm-Leach-Bliley Act (GLBA)*, by David H. Carpenter and M. Maureen Murphy.

---

financial business, echoing Glass-Steagall's separation of banking and investing.[68] Reintroducing the separation of lines of business alone would not necessarily prevent the existence of very large or interconnected firms within a market segment, however, in which case the TBTF problem would not be eliminated.

The benefits of reducing the scope of firms are that, if successful, it could reduce the riskiest activities of large firms and thus the need for future "bailouts" stemming from TBTF. It could also reduce the complexity of large firms, making it easier for regulators and creditors to monitor them. Weighed against those benefits would be a number of costs.

First, there may be economies of scope that make the financial system more efficient and complete if firms are large, diversified, and interconnected. Customers may benefit from the convenience, sophistication, and savings of "one-stop shopping" and expertise in multiple market segments.

Second, large firms that operate in multiple lines of business may be better able to reduce risk through diversification, making them less prone to instability in that sense. Traditional banking is not inherently safe, so forbidding banks from engaging in other activities is no panacea to avoid bank failures. Fannie Mae and Freddie Mac are examples of firms that were deemed "too big to fail" and rescued on those grounds although their business was narrowly focused in the mortgage market.

Third, reintroducing Glass-Steagall separations of businesses without other changes to the regulatory system would reinforce a system in which banking is subject to close federal prudential regulation and other financial firms are not. This system would only mitigate systemic risk if non-banking activities and institutions could not be a source of systemic risk—the recent crisis experience casts doubt on that assumption. Further, the growth in "shadow banking" makes it more difficult to segregate activities and their regulation by charter—financial innovation has blurred the distinction between different lines of business in finance to the point where the distinction may not be meaningful. In other words, some activities of non-banks are not fundamentally different from core banking activities from an economic perspective. Thus, the activities that banks could undertake would be limited, but it would be difficult to prevent non-banks from engaging in bank-like activities with the same implications for systemic risk, but less or no prudential regulation. Similar arguments apply to the potential for activities to migrate abroad, where "universal banking" is common.

Another policy approach would be to limit or ban TBTF firms' participation in activities that are deemed inherently too risky—particularly those likely to generate large losses at times of financial stress—and not central to the business model of the firm. This approach usually focuses on banks because of their access to the "federal safety net" (deposit insurance and Fed lending), and hence justified in terms of limiting risk to taxpayers. For example, many policy makers have argued that banks should not participate in proprietary trading of private securities with the bank's own funds.[69] Although all financial activities are risky, some risks can be more easily managed through techniques such as hedging and supervised by regulators. Whether proprietary trading is

---

[68] Under current law, there are still limits on the types of business activities that banking subsidiaries can undertake, but non-banking subsidiaries within the same holding company may operate in different lines of financial business.

[69] Financial Stability Oversight Council, *Study and Recommendations on Prohibitions on Proprietary Trading*, January 2011, http://www.treasury.gov/initiatives/Documents/Volcker%20sec%20%20619%20study%20final%201%2018%2011%20rg.pdf.

---

an inherently riskier activity than other banking functions, such as lending, is subject to debate. In addition to proprietary trading, Thomas Hoenig and Charles Morris have proposed to also ban banks from acting as broker-dealers and market-makers in securities and derivatives.[70]

Another variation of this proposal, made by the Vickers Commission in the United Kingdom[71] and the Liikanen Group in the European Union,[72] is to "ring fence" banking activities from these other types of activities into legally, financially, and operationally separate entities within a holding company structure.[73] This type of approach can be seen in U.S. policies to move swap dealer activities outside of the depository subsidiary and into a separately capitalized subsidiary (referred to as "the swap push out rule").[74] Similarly to proprietary trading, a challenge to this approach is to differentiate between derivatives activities that regulators want depository subsidiaries to engage in, such as risk-mitigating hedging, and the targeted activities, such as swap dealing.

Although proposals limiting scope would apply to both large and small banks, some are likely to have a greater impact on large firms. For example, Bloomberg Government estimates that over 99% of trading assets and liabilities are held by 25 banks.[75]

A drawback to limiting permissible activities is that there is unlikely to be any sharp distinction between the risky activity and similar activities that are central to the firm's core activities. As a result, regulators may have to make arbitrary distinctions between which activities fall under the ban, and firms would have an incentive to skirt the ban by designing transactions that resemble allowed activities but accomplish the same goals as the banned activity. For example, proprietary trading ("playing the market" with a firm's own assets) may be hard to distinguish from market-making (providing clients with a ready buyer and seller of securities) or hedging (buying and selling securities such as derivatives to reduce risk), and there may be economies of scale to market-making that concentrate those activities at large firms.[76] Finally, risky activities may still be a source of systemic risk even if banks or TBTFs are banned from conducting them.

Policy Response

Section 619 of the Dodd-Frank Act, popularly referred to as the "Volcker Rule," prohibits banks from engaging in proprietary trading and owning hedge funds and private equity funds in the United States, and requires additional capital to be held by systemically important non-banks that

---

[70] Thomas Hoenig and Charles Morris, "Restructuring the Banking System to Improve Safety and Soundness," Federal Reserve Bank of Kansas City, working paper, December 2012.

[71] Independent Commission on Banking, *Interim Report*, United Kingdom, April 2011.

[72] High-level Expert Group on Reforming the Structure of the EU banking Sector Chaired by Erkki Liikanen, *Final Report*, European Union, October 2, 2012.

[73] In the United States, some have argued that each subsidiary within a holding company should be made legally and operationally separate. See, for example, Sheila Bair, *Bull by the Horns*, Simon and Schuster, (New York, NY: 2012), p. 329; Brad Miller, "Use Stand-Alone Subsidiaries to Break Up Megabanks," *Wall Street Journal*, October 21, 2012.

[74] The term swaps refers to over-the-counter derivatives. It is statutorily defined in 7 USC 1a(47).

[75] Cady North, "Volcker Rule Risk Concentrated in 25 Banks," Bloomberg Government, October 14, 2011, p. 5.

[76] See American Bankers Association, *Letter to Alastair Fitzpayne: Information on the FSOC Notice 2010-0002*, November 3, 2010, http://www.aba.com/aba/documents/news/VolckerTrust11410.pdf; SIFMA, *Volcker Rule*, http://www.sifma.org/issues/regulatory-reform/volcker-rule/position/.

engage in proprietary trading or own hedge funds and private equity funds in the United States.[77] Insurance companies are excluded from the Volcker Rule. Exemptions from the Volcker Rule include the purchase and sale of assets for purposes of underwriting, market making, hedging, and on behalf of clients. Securities issued by federal, state, or local governments and government-sponsored enterprises (GSEs) are exempted, as are investments in small business investment companies. A final rule implementing the Volcker Rule was adopted in December 2013, with conformance required by June 2015.[78]

Section 716 of the Dodd-Frank Act requires banks to "push out" certain swap dealer activities into separately capitalized affiliates.[79] The stated goal of the provision is to prevent swap dealers and major swap participants from accessing deposit insurance or the Fed's discount window. The rule implementing Section 716 was effective July 2013, with a two-year transition period.[80]

Regulating TBTF

Options

Another approach to addressing the TBTF problem takes as its starting point that no policy can prevent TBTF firms from emerging. In this view, the dominant role of a few firms in key segments of the financial system is unavoidable. Breaking them up or eliminating all spillover effects is unlikely to be practical or feasible, for reasons discussed elsewhere. If so, regulation could be used to try to counteract the moral hazard problem and reduce the likelihood of their failure. Prudential regulation, such as capital requirements, could be set to hold TBTF firms to higher standards than other financial firms, whether or not those firms are already subject to prudential regulation.

A framework for prudential regulation is well established in depository banking regulation, featuring the setting of safety and soundness standards and regulatory supervision to ensure adherence to those standards. Historically, banks have been subject to a closer and more intense federal prudential regulatory regime than non-banks because of the systemic risk and moral hazard problems they posed. Some argue that banks generate unique sources of systemic risk (such as deposit taking) that have no analogue in other types of financial firms.[81] If the recent crisis leads to the conclusion that TBTF non-bank financial firms can also be sources of systemic risk and contagion, the same arguments made for regulating banks for systemic risk also apply to TBTF non-banks, however.[82]

---

[77] For more information, see CRS Report R41298, *The "Volcker Rule": Proposals to Limit "Speculative" Proprietary Trading by Banks*, by David H. Carpenter and M. Maureen Murphy.

[78] Available at http://federalreserve.gov/newsevents/press/bcreg/20131210a htm.

[79] For more information, see CRS Report R41398, *The Dodd-Frank Wall Street Reform and Consumer Protection Act: Title VII, Derivatives*, by Rena S. Miller and Kathleen Ann Ruane.

[80] Available at http://federalreserve.gov/newsevents/press/bcreg/20130605a htm.

[81] The potential for each type of financial firm to be a source of systemic risk is evaluated in Douglas Elliot, "Regulating Systemically Important Financial Institutions That Are Not Banks," Brookings Institution, working paper, May 9, 2013, available at http://www.brookings.edu/research/papers/2013/05/09-regulating-financial-institutions-elliott.

[82] Whether all non-bank firms or only TBTF ones performing a given financial activity are important sources of systemic risk is beyond the scope of this report, but if all were, a case could be made that a prudential regulatory regime should be applied uniformly to all such firms, and not just large ones.

There are a wide variety of types of large non-banks, with diverse features. Some non-banks have some of the features that have been viewed as a source of systemic risk, such as leverage and vulnerability to runs, while others do not. There are a few large insurers, which are already regulated for safety and soundness at the state level. On the other hand, state regulators may not be equipped to regulate non-insurance subsidiaries or the overall firm for systemic risk. A study by the Office of Financial Research (OFR) identified several channels through which "asset managers"—a diverse group that includes hedge funds, pension funds, and mutual funds—could pose systemic risks. Others have argued that only activities, not firms, in this industry pose systemic risk. The OFR report identified 10 asset managers each with more than $1 trillion in assets under management.[83]

A "one size fits all" model for regulating firms in different businesses for safety and soundness is unlikely to be practical. Bringing non-banks under the purview of bank regulators raises questions about whether rules designed for banks can be applied to non-banks, and whether the federal bank regulators have the expertise to do so effectively. For example, insurers have argued that bank regulations are not suitable for them and the Fed does not have any specialized expertise in the area of insurance. Another issue is whether to regulate all of the activities of holding companies operating across several lines of business for safety and soundness, or regulate only certain activities that are deemed systemically important, perhaps with legal and financial "firewalls" that isolate the risks of non-regulated activities to the overall holding company.

Regulation cannot prevent all failures from occurring—large, regulated depository institutions failed during the crisis. Nor is a system without any failures necessarily a desirable one, since risk is inherent in all financial activities. Regulation could aim to prevent large financial firms from taking greater risks than their smaller counterparts because of moral hazard. If successful, fewer failures or episodes involving disruptive losses would occur. If effective, monitoring by regulators might be more economically efficient than monitoring by creditors and counterparties, where a free rider problem reduces the incentive to monitor. In addition, regulators potentially have greater access to relevant information on risk than creditors and counterparties if opacity is a problem with large, complex firms.

This proposal relies on effective regulation by the same regulators who were arguably unable or unwilling to prevent excessive risk taking before and during the crisis by at least a few of the firms that they regulated.[84] Although regulation is intended to limit risky behavior, regulators may inadvertently cause greater correlation of losses across firms by encouraging all firms to engage in similar behavior. Some have argued that large firms are "too complex to regulate," meaning regulators are incapable of identifying or understanding the risks inherent in complicated transactions and corporate structures. For example, the six largest BHCs had more than 1,000 subsidiaries and the two largest had more than 3,000 each in 2012. Further, their complexity has increased over time—only one BHC had more than 500 subsidiaries in 1990, and the share of assets held outside of depository subsidiaries has grown over time for the largest BHCs.[85] One

---

[83] See Office of Financial Research, *Asset Management and Financial Stability*, September 2013, http://www.treasury.gov/initiatives/ofr/research/Documents/OFR_AMFS_FINAL.pdf; Douglas Elliott, "Systemic Risk and the Asset Management Industry," Brookings Institution, May 2014.

[84] This is discussed in more detail in the **Appendix**. See also Arthur Wilmarth, "The Dodd-Frank Act: A Flawed and Inadequate Response to the Too-Big-To-Fail Problem," *Oregon Law Review*, vol. 89, April 6, 2011, p. 951.

[85] Dafna Avraham, et al., "Peeling the Onion: A Structural View of U.S. Bank Holding Companies," *Liberty Street Economics*, July 20, 2012, available at http://libertystreeteconomics newyorkfed.org/2012/07/peeling-the-onion-a-structural-view-of-us-bank-holding-companies.html#.U-TnELFgi68.

response to addressing this complexity is by making the regulatory regime more sophisticated, but some critics argue that this approach is likely to backfire.[86] One challenge for the effective regulation of non-banks that are TBTF is that regulators have less experience with business lines other than banking, and thus may initially lack the expertise to regulate them effectively. Others have argued that large firms are "too big to jail," meaning regulators cannot take effective supervisory actions against firms if those actions would undermine the firm's financial health, and thus financial stability.[87]

One way that a regulatory approach could potentially backfire is if a special regulatory regime for TBTF firms is not strict enough, in which case it would exacerbate the moral hazard problem. Critics fear that such a regime would be particularly vulnerable to "regulatory capture," the phenomenon in which the regulated exercise influence over their regulators to ease the burden of regulation. If so, a special regulatory regime could wind up exacerbating the moral hazard problem by, in effect, making TBTF status explicit, signaling to market participants that firms in the special regime enjoyed a protected status and would not be allowed to fail.[88] Instead of increasing the cost of being TBTF, firms in the special regulatory regime could end up borrowing at a lower cost than other firms (since, in effect, these firms would enjoy a lower risk of default).

Many would point to the experience with the GSEs, Fannie Mae and Freddie Mac, before conservatorship as a historical example of how a special regulatory regime could backfire. The GSEs could borrow at a lower cost than other firms because markets believed that the government would not let them fail—they enjoyed even lower borrowing costs than firms that markets might believe were implicitly TBTF but not chartered by the government like the GSEs.[89] Institutional shortcomings, critics argue, led to regulatory capture.[90] The GSEs were subject to their own unique capital requirements, set by statute, under which they were found well capitalized by their regulator at the time, OFHEO, two months before being taken into conservatorship.[91] Yet compared with depositories, GSEs held little capital, were not well diversified, and experienced large losses during the crisis. The worst-case scenario of opponents of a separate regulatory regime for TBTF firms is that such a regime would provide a competitive advantage that would enable more risk taking than before. An example of this scenario was the GSEs' ability to borrow at lower cost than other firms.

Adopting these measures may increase overall costs in the financial system, but in the presence of TBTF, market costs may otherwise be too low from a societal perspective, since risk-taking is too high. For example, requiring loans to be backed with more capital may make lending more expensive and less available, but make the firm less likely to fail. If more capital succeeded in creating a more stable financial system, then the availability of credit could be less volatile over

---

[86] See, for example, Thomas Hoenig, "Back to Basics: A Better Alternative to Basel Capital Rules," Federal Deposit Insurance Corporation, speech delivered to the American Banker Regulatory Symposium, September 14, 2012.

[87] This issue was discussed by the Attorney General at a 2013 hearing. See U.S. Congress, Senate Judiciary Committee, *Oversight of the U.S. Department of Justice*, 113th Cong., 1st sess., March 6, 2013.

[88] During the debate of the Dodd-Frank Act, policy makers considered keeping the identities of regulated firms confidential, but they concluded that this would be impractical.

[89] Congressional Budget Office, *Measuring the Capital Positions of Fannie Mae and Freddie Mac*, June 2006.

[90] For an in-depth discussion, see the section in the Appendix entitled "Fannie Mae and Freddie Mac."

[91] Office of Federal Housing Enterprise Oversight, "Fannie Mae and Freddie Mac Capital," *Mortgage Market Note 08-2*, July 17, 2008.

time. At least partly offsetting the higher costs of capital for firms designated as systemically important would be relatively lower costs of capital for other firms.[92]

Even if a heightened prudential regime worked as planned, it could still partly backfire from a systemic risk perspective. To the extent that it causes financial intermediation to migrate away from TBTF firms to firms that are not regulated for safety and soundness, the result could be a less regulated financial system.

Policy Response

Title I of the Dodd-Frank Act grants the Financial Stability Oversight Council (FSOC) the authority to identify "systemically important" non-bank financial firms (SIFI) by a two-thirds vote, which must be supported by the Treasury Secretary. Such a firm would be deemed systemically important on the basis of a council determination that "material financial distress at the [firm] or the nature, scope, size, scale, concentration, interconnectedness, or mix of the activities of the [firm] could pose a threat to the financial stability of the United States." Foreign financial firms operating in the United States could be identified by the council as systemically important. Firms with consolidated assets of less than $50 billion are exempted. Besides the $50 billion threshold, FSOC stated in its final rule that it would consider designating only firms with at least $30 billion in gross notional credit default swaps outstanding in which it was the reference entity, $3.5 billion of derivatives liabilities, $20 billion in debt outstanding, a 15 to 1 leverage ratio (a capital-asset ratio that is not risk-weighted), or a 10% short-term debt ratio.[93]

To date, FSOC has designated two insurers (AIG and Prudential) and another non-bank (GE Capital) as SIFIs.[94] According to the insurer MetLife, FSOC has proposed to designate it as well.[95] FSOC has investigated whether any "asset managers" (a diverse group that includes mutual funds, hedge funds, and private equity funds) are systemically important, but has not made any designations to date.

Under Subtitle C of Title I, the Fed is the prudential regulator for firms that the FSOC has designated as a SIFI and any BHC with total consolidated assets of $50 billion. (The FSOC and Fed may raise the asset threshold above $50 billion.) There are currently about 30 U.S. BHCs with more than $50 billion in consolidated assets.[96] BHCs that participated in the Capital Purchase Program (part of the Troubled Asset Relief Program) would not be able to change their

---

[92] Assuming that the overall supply of credit remained constant, raising the cost of capital at TBTF firms would reduce the amount of credit supplied to those firms, thereby increasing the supply of credit available to other firms. Economic theory predicts that the greater supply of credit available to other firms would reduce their cost of capital.

[93] FSOC issued a final rule in April 2012. It can be accessed at http://www.treasury.gov/initiatives/fsoc/rulemaking/ Documents/ Authority%20to%20Require%20Supervision%20and%20Regulation%20of%20Certain%20Nonbank%20Financial%20 Companies.pdf.

[94] Financial Stability Oversight Council, "Council Names Two Companies for Consolidated Supervision and Enhanced Prudential Standards," *press release*, July 9, 2013.

[95] MetLife, press release, September 4, 2014, https://www metlife.com/about/press-room/index html?compID=140852.

[96] A current list of top 50 depositories by asset size is available at http://www.ffiec.gov/nicpubweb/nicweb/ Top50Form.aspx. Some of the firms on this list are not bank holding companies. Other types of depositories, such as savings and loan holding companies, with more than $50 billion in assets are not subject to the final rule, but the Fed has indicated that it intends to propose rulemaking in the future that apply to them. There are no official data on the largest financial firms that are not depositories.

charter to avoid this regulatory regime. A large number of foreign banks operating in the United States are also subject to the enhanced prudential regime.[97] Foreign banks operating with more than $50 billion in assets in the United States are required to set up intermediate bank holding companies that will be subject to heightened standards comparable to those applied to U.S. banks. Less stringent requirements apply to large foreign banks with less than $50 billion in assets in the United States. The Fed, with the FSOC's advice, is required to set safety and soundness standards that are more stringent than those applicable to other nonbank financial firms and BHCs that do not pose a systemic risk. At the recommendation of the council or on its own initiative, the Fed may set different standards for different systemically important firms or categories of firms based on various risk-related factors. Fees are assessed on banks and non-banks regulated under this regime to finance the costs of supervision, as well as the budget of the Office of Financial Research.

The final rule implementing Subtitle C was adopted in February 2014, and banks must be in compliance by January 1, 2015.[98] The final rule includes requirements for stress tests, capital planning, and risk management. The final rule also requires any bank with more than $50 billion in assets to comply with a 15 to 1 debt to equity limit in the event that the FSOC has determined that it poses a "grave threat" to financial stability. Exposure limits of 25% of a company's capital per single counterparty were included in the proposed rule, but the Fed has indicated that it plans to finalize them at a later date. Capital and liquidity standards for the largest banks have been set separately through the Basel III rules, discussed below; enhanced capital requirements have not been required of all BHCs with $50 billion or more in assets. Other prudential standards may be applied at the Fed's discretion.

In addition, Section 171 of the Dodd-Frank Act (the "Collins Amendment") requires the Fed to set capital requirements at the holding company level for non-bank SIFIs and all bank or savings and loan holding companies that are no lower than those applied to banking subsidiaries. For companies with small or no banking subsidiaries, most of the required capital may be based on the activities of and provided by the non-bank subsidiaries. Previously, capital requirements (if there were any) were determined at the subsidiary level by that subsidiary's primary regulator. There are various exceptions to and phase-in periods for this requirement, including an exemption for small holding companies. As BHC regulator, the Fed has not yet determined how to apply the Collins Amendment to insurers, who use different methods to measure capital requirements from banks, or other non-banks.

In conjunction with the Dodd-Frank Act, Basel III, a non-binding international agreement on bank regulation that the United States is in the process of implementing,[99] required that

> global systemically important financial institutions (SIFIs) must have higher loss absorbency capacity to reflect the greater risks that they pose to the financial system. The Committee has developed a methodology that includes both quantitative indicators and qualitative elements to identify global systemically important banks (G-SIBs). The additional loss absorbency

---

[97] CRS was not able to locate an official list of banks subject to Title I enhanced supervision. About 130 banks (foreign and domestic) have submitted resolution plans ("living wills") pursuant to Title I, however. See Martin Gruenberg, testimony before the Senate Committee on Banking, Housing, and Urban Affairs, September 9, 2014, p. 5.

[98] The rule can be accessed at http://federalreserve.gov/newsevents/press/bcreg/20140218a htm.

[99] Many provisions of the Basel III Accord were adopted in rulemaking in July 2013. The 2013 final rule does not include the capital surcharge for G-SIBs, which regulators have announced will be proposed at a later date. For more information, see http://federalreserve.gov/bankinforeg/basel/USImplementation htm.

---

requirements are to be met with a progressive Common Equity Tier 1 (CET1) capital requirement ranging from 1% to 2.5%, depending on a bank's systemic importance. For banks facing the highest SIB surcharge, an additional loss absorbency of 1% could be applied as a disincentive to increase materially their global systemic importance in the future.[100]

In addition, Basel III creates a counter-cyclical capital buffer that can be modified over the business cycle and a supplementary leverage ratio incorporating off-balance sheet assets, both of which will be applied to only the largest banks (specifically, those subject to the "Advanced Approaches" Rule). In September 2014, the banking regulators finalized a rule implementing Basel's liquidity coverage ratio, applying it to banks with $250 billion or more in assets or $10 billion or more in on-balance sheet exposure, and a less stringent version of the rule to banks with $50 billion or more in assets. The rule does not apply to non-bank SIFIs, but regulators indicated that non-bank SIFIs would face their own liquidity requirements. The liquidity coverage ratio would require firms to hold enough liquid assets to meet cash flow needs during a stress period.[101]

Since 2011, the Financial Stability Board (FSB), an international forum that coordinates the work of national financial authorities and international standard setting bodies, has annually designated G-SIBs, based on the banks' cross-jurisdictional activity, size, interconnectedness, substitutability, and complexity.[102] The FSB has currently designated 29 banks as G-SIBs. **Table 2** lists the eight G-SIBs that are headquartered in the United States, and the capital surcharge under Basel III recommended by the FSB. In addition, several of the foreign G-SIBs have U.S. subsidiaries. The identified firms are required to meet resolution planning requirements.[103] The FSB has proposed that firms identified as G-SIBs in 2014 meet the capital surcharge requirements beginning in 2016, fully phasing them in by January 2019. The G20, including the U.S. government, endorsed the FSB's non-binding proposal.

Table 2. U.S. Banks Identified as G-SIBs and Capital Surcharge Recommended by the FSB

(surcharge as a % of risk-weighted assets)

U.S. Financial Firm	Capital Surcharge as a % of Risk-Weighted Assets
Citigroup	2.5%
JP Morgan Chase	2.5%
Bank of America	1.5%
Bank of New York Mellon	1.5%
Goldman Sachs	1.5%
Morgan Stanley	1.5%

[100] Bank for International Settlements, *Basel III Summary Table*, http://www.bis.org/bcbs/basel3/b3summarytable.pdf.

[101] The final rule can be accessed here: http://federalreserve.gov/newsevents/press/bcreg/bcreg20140903a1.pdf.

[102] Financial Stability Board, "Policy Measures to Address Systemically Important Financial Institutions," November 4, 2011, http://www.financialstabilityboard.org/publications/r_111104bb.pdf. The identification methodology is described in Basel Committee on Banking Supervision, "Global Systemically Important Banks: Assessment Methodology," *Consultative Document*, July 2011, http://www.bis.org/publ/bcbs201.pdf.

[103] Financial Stability Board, "2013 Update of Global Systemically Important Banks," November 11, 2013, http://www.financialstabilityboard.org/publications/r_131111.pdf.

U.S. Financial Firm	Capital Surcharge as a % of Risk-Weighted Assets
State Street	1.0%
Wells Fargo	1.0%

Source: Financial Stability Board.

In April 2014, the U.S. bank regulators adopted a joint rule that would require these eight banks to meet a supplementary leverage ratio of 5% in order to pay all discretionary bonuses and capital distributions and 6% in order to be considered well capitalized as of 2018.[104] The supplementary leverage ratio includes off-balance sheet exposures.

In addition, the Financial Stability Board has identified nine insurers as "globally systemically important insurers," three of whom (AIG, Prudential, and MetLife) are headquartered in the United States.[105] Designated insurers will be required to develop recovery and resolution plans and hold more capital than other insurers by 2019. The FSB has released a methodology for identifying global systemically important firms that are not banks or insurers, but has not designated any to date.[106] Some Members of Congress have been concerned that the FSB designation process is superseding the national designation process established by the Dodd-Frank Act.[107]

Minimize Spillover Effects

Options

A criticism of regulation before the crisis was that regulators did not focus enough on how a firm's failure would affect its counterparties or broader financial conditions, or conversely, whether a firm could withstand a crisis situation. Another approach holds that if firms are TBTF because their failure would cause spillover effects that would impair the overall financial system, then instead of altering the TBTF firm, regulators should try to neutralize spillover effects to the point where the failure of a firm would not impair the broader financial system. According to this view, once creditors believed that a firm could now safely be allowed to fail regardless of its size or interconnectedness, the moral hazard problem associated with TBTF would vanish.

One way spillover effects occur is through counterparty risk (the risk of losses because a counterparty in a transaction cannot fulfill its obligations). Examples of how counterparty risk can be reduced include moving transactions to clearinghouses and exchanges, requiring capital/margins for transactions, requiring risk exposures to be hedged, and placing limits on

---

[104] The rule applies to all banks with more than $700 billion in assets, and was set at that level to include all banks designated as G-SIBs. The rule can be viewed at http://federalreserve.gov/newsevents/press/bcreg/20140408a htm.

[105] Financial Stability Board, "Global Systemically Important Insurers and the Policy Measures That Will Apply to Them," July 18, 2013, http://www.financialstabilityboard.org/publications/r_130718.pdf. The Financial Stability Board is an international forum of which the United States is a member. A list of the U.S. firms can be found in the section below entitled "Regulating TBTF."

[106] Financial Stability Board, "Assessment Methodologies for Identifying Non-Bank Non-Insurer Global Systemically Important Financial Institutions," January 8, 2014, http://www.financialstabilityboard.org/publications/r_140108 htm.

[107] Hon. Jeb Hensarling et al, "Letter to Secretary Lew, Chair White, and Chair Yellen," May 9, 2014.

---

exposure to specific counterparties (transactions, debt, equity holdings, etc.).[108] Adopting these measures may increase overall costs in the financial system. For example, counterparty limits could reduce liquidity and raise costs for transactions that are not standardized enough to be traded on exchanges. In the presence of TBTF, however, market costs may otherwise be too low from a society-wide perspective, because firms lack the proper incentives to monitor or price in counterparty risk.

A drawback to this approach is that spillover effects cannot always be identified beforehand. If counterparty exposure were transparent, in theory all market participants could hedge themselves against failure ahead of time and the failure would not have contagion effects, or at least the government could manage the exposure to prevent contagion. In practice, linkages have proven complex and opaque, and the sources of contagion have proven hard to predict. For example, in September 2008, policy makers reasoned that market participants and policy makers had had several months after the rescue of Bear Stearns to prepare for the failure of Lehman Brothers (indicators such as credit default swaps had signaled an elevated risk of default for months), so allowing it to enter bankruptcy should not be disruptive.[109] Nevertheless, few anticipated that Lehman Brothers' failure would lead to a run on money markets, which proved highly disruptive to commercial paper markets, causing financing problems for many financial and non-financial issuers.

Identifying spillover effects is likely to be more difficult if a firm is not already regulated for safety and soundness. Without a prudential regulator closely monitoring the firm's activities and examining its counterparties, it is less likely that policy makers could quickly and accurately identify who would be exposed to a firm's failure. Much of the necessary information to make that judgment is unlikely to be publicly available.

Another problem is that some solutions shift, rather than eliminate, counterparty risk. For example, moving certain activities onto an exchange or clearinghouse may cause that entity to become "too interconnected to fail."

Policy Response

The Federal Reserve's Regulation F (12 C.F.R., Part 206)—in place before the crisis—limits counterparty exposure for depository institutions. Title I of the Dodd-Frank Act allows the Fed to set exposure limits of 25% of a company's capital per counterparty for firms designated as systemically important by the Financial Stability Oversight Council.[110] To date, a rule implementing this exposure limit has been proposed but not finalized. To reduce counterparty risk, Title VII of the Dodd-Frank Act requires certain swaps, particularly those that involve large financial institutions, to be moved onto clearinghouses or exchanges.[111] Title VIII of the Dodd-Frank Act allows the Financial Stability Oversight Council to identify certain payment, clearing, and settlement systems and activities as systemically important "financial market utilities," and

---

[108] Gary Stern and Ron Feldman, *Too Big to Fail* (Washington, DC: Brookings Institution Press), 2004.

[109] An alternative view is that Lehman Brothers' bankruptcy was more disruptive because the rescue of Bear Stearns led creditors to conclude that other large investment banks would also be rescued.

[110] The Fed has issued a proposed rule to implement these standards, which can be accessed at http://www.federalreserve.gov/newsevents/press/bcreg/bcreg20111220a1.pdf.

[111] For more information, see CRS Report R41398, *The Dodd-Frank Wall Street Reform and Consumer Protection Act: Title VII, Derivatives*, by Rena S. Miller and Kathleen Ann Ruane.

allows the Federal Reserve, Securities and Exchange Commission, or Commodity and Futures Trading Commission to regulate those systems and activities for enhanced prudential supervision. It also allows systemically important systems to borrow from the Fed in "unusual or exigent circumstances." In 2012, regulators issued a final rule implementing Title VIII and designated eight financial market utilities as systemically important.[112]

Resolving a Large, Interconnected Failing Firm

Options

Prior to the financial crisis, failing banks were resolved through the FDIC's resolution regime, while certain other financial firms, such as broker-dealers, were resolved through the corporate bankruptcy system.[113] Bankruptcy is a judicial process initiated by creditors in order to recover debts and other liabilities, while the FDIC's resolution regime is an administrative process initiated by the FDIC. Examples of the types of powers that the FDIC can exercise to resolve a depository include transferring and freezing assets, paying obligations, repudiating contracts, and obtaining judicial stays.[114]

The FDIC typically resolves failed banks through the "purchase and assumption" method, under which the bank is closed and some or all of the assets and deposits of the failed bank are sold to healthy banks.[115] If losses are too large to be absorbed by creditors, they are absorbed by the FDIC's deposit insurance fund, which is pre-funded through assessments on depositories. The purchase and assumption method avoids open-ended government assistance and keeps the FDIC out of the business of running banks, but an unintended consequence is that it encourages greater concentration, since the only entity capable of absorbing a large failed bank is likely to be an even larger institution.

One rationale behind a resolution regime for banks is that the need to safeguard federally insured deposits (which can be withdrawn rapidly) requires a swift resolution and gives the FDIC, which insures the deposits, priority over other creditors. Prompt corrective action and least cost resolution requirements are intended to minimize losses to the FDIC. The FDIC may initiate a resolution before failure has occurred—thereby limiting losses to the FDIC and other creditors— whereas a bankruptcy process cannot be initiated by creditors until default has occurred.

Another example of a resolution regime is the one applied to Fannie Mae and Freddie Mac. Their regulator, the Federal Housing Finance Agency (FHFA), assumed control of Fannie Mae and Freddie Mac in September 2008 when FHFA determined that they were critically undercapitalized. Since then, Fannie Mae and Freddie Mac have operated under government

---

[112] For more information, see CRS Report R41529, *Supervision of U.S. Payment, Clearing, and Settlement Systems: Designation of Financial Market Utilities (FMUs)*, by Marc Labonte.

[113] For more information, see CRS Report R40530, *Insolvency of Systemically Significant Financial Companies (SSFCs): Bankruptcy vs. Conservatorship/Receivership*, by David H. Carpenter.

[114] See CRS Report RL34657, *Financial Institution Insolvency: Federal Authority over Fannie Mae, Freddie Mac, and Depository Institutions*, by David H. Carpenter and M. Maureen Murphy.

[115] For more information on purchase and assumption and other resolution methods, see the section below entitled "Resolution of Banks Before and After the Federal Deposit Insurance Corporation Improvement Act."

conservatorship and received quarterly financial transfers from the Treasury to remain solvent until 2012.[116]

Part of what makes some financial firms too big to fail is the nature of the bankruptcy process, according to some analysts. A firm that dominates important financial market segments cannot be liquidated without disrupting the availability of credit, it is argued. They argue that the deliberate pace of the bankruptcy process is not equipped to avoid the runs and contagion inherent in the failure of a financial firm, and that the effects on systemic risk are not taken into account when decisions are made in the bankruptcy process. The bankruptcy experience of Lehman Brothers is viewed as evidence of why the current bankruptcy process cannot be successful for a TBTF firm.

Proponents argue that a resolution regime for all TBTF financial firms, regardless of whether the firm is a depository, offers an alternative to propping up failing firms with government assistance (as was the case with Bear Stearns and AIG in 2008) or suffering the systemic consequences of a protracted and messy bankruptcy (as was the case with Lehman Brothers).[117] In principle, a TBTF resolution regime could include a receivership process (where the government seizes control of the firm in order to wind it down), a conservatorship process (where the government seizes control in order to continue operations), or both. The FDIC's typical treatment of a failed bank is an example of a receivership process; FHFA's treatment of Fannie Mae and Freddie Mac since 2008 is an example of the conservatorship process.[118] Often, banks in receivership are resolved through acquisitions by healthy firms. In the case of a large firm, acquisitions would result in the acquiring firm becoming even larger. Were one of the nation's very largest firms to fail, it is not clear what firm would have the capacity to acquire it, in which case some other method of resolution would be necessary.

Supporting the argument for a special resolution regime, the failures of large depositories during the crisis that were subject to the FDIC's resolution regime, such as Wachovia and Washington Mutual, were less disruptive to the financial system than the failure of Lehman Brothers, even though Wachovia and Lehman Brothers were sequential (46th and 47th largest, respectively) on *Fortune*'s list of the 500 largest companies of 2007.[119] (Wells Fargo acquired Wachovia before the FDIC formally became receiver.) Whether the resolution of a non-bank could be handled as smoothly as these two banks is an open question.[120]

Critics argue that a resolution regime, depending on its design, could give policy makers too much discretionary power, which could result in higher costs to the government and preferential treatment of favored creditors during the resolution. In other words, it could enable "backdoor bailouts" that could allow government assistance to be funneled to the firm or its creditors beyond

---

[116] For more information, see the section below entitled "Fannie Mae and Freddie Mac."

[117] See, for example, Sheila Bair, "We Must Resolve to End Too Big to Fail," remarks at the 47th Annual Conference on Bank Structure and Competition, Federal Reserve Bank of Chicago, May 5, 2011, http://www.fdic.gov/bank/analytical/quarterly/2011_vol5_2/Article1.pdf.

[118] For more information, see CRS Report RS22950, *Fannie Mae and Freddie Mac in Conservatorship*, by Mark Jickling.

[119] For more information, see "Washington Mutual and Wachovia." The Fortune list can be accessed at http://money.cnn.com/magazines/fortune/fortune500/2007/full_list/index.html.

[120] The FDIC gives a detailed explanation of how the failure of a firm like Lehman Brothers could have been managed more smoothly under a resolution regime in "The Orderly Liquidation of Lehman Brothers Holdings Under the Dodd-Frank Act," *FDIC Quarterly*, vol. 5, no. 2, 2011, p. 31, http://www.fdic.gov/bank/analytical/quarterly/2011_vol5_2/lehman.pdf.

what would be available in bankruptcy, perpetuating the moral hazard problem.[121] The normal FDIC resolution regime minimizes the potential for these problems through its statutory requirements of least cost resolution and prompt corrective action. It would be expected that a resolution regime for TBTF firms, by contrast, would at times be required to subordinate a least cost principle to systemic risk considerations, which the FDIC regime permits. Therefore, a resolution could be more costly to the government than the bankruptcy process. (On the other hand, an administrative resolution process could potentially avoid some of the costs of bankruptcy, such as some legal fees and runs by creditors that further undermine the firm's finances.) Critics also point to the conservatorship of Fannie Mae and Freddie Mac—who have received government support on an ongoing basis since 2008—as evidence that a resolution regime could turn out to be too open ended and be used to prop up TBTF firms as ongoing entities, competing with private sector rivals on an advantageous basis because of direct government subsidies. The Housing and Economic Recovery Act (P.L. 110-289) required mandatory receivership for the GSEs if they became insolvent, but quarterly transfers from Treasury prevented insolvency. As noted above, uncertainty before the fact about which firms are TBTF may lead policy makers to err on the side of taking more failing firms than necessary into the special resolution process instead of allowing them to enter bankruptcy.

If policy makers, wary of the turmoil caused by Lehman Brothers' failure, were unwilling to pursue the bankruptcy option in the future, opposing a resolution regime may be tantamount to tacitly accepting future "bailouts," unless some other policy change is made that future policy makers view as a workable alternative. As an alternative to a special resolution regime, some critics call for amending the bankruptcy code to create a special chapter for complex financial firms to address problems that have been identified, such as a speedier process and the ability to reorganize.[122] To some extent, these concerns are already addressed in the bankruptcy code. For example, the bankruptcy process already allows qualified financial contracts to be netted out. In the case of Lehman Brothers, healthy business units were sold to competitors relatively quickly through the bankruptcy process, and remain in operation today.

Until a TBTF firm fails, it is open to debate whether a special resolution regime could successfully achieve what it is intended to do—shut down a failing firm without triggering systemic disruption. One key challenge that has been identified is the resolution of foreign subsidiaries.[123] Given the size of the firms involved and the unanticipated transmission of systemic risk, it remains to be seen whether the government could impose losses on any creditors without triggering contagion—or would be willing to try. A receiver would face the same short-term incentives to limit losses to creditors to limit systemic risk that caused policy makers to rescue firms in the recent crisis in order to restore stability. If the receiver is guided by those short-term incentives, the only difference between a resolution regime and a "bailout" might turn out to be that shareholder equity is wiped out, at presumably relatively little savings to the government.

---

[121] See, for example, Jeffrey Lacker and John Weinberg, "Now How Large is the Safety Net?" *Economic Brief 10-06*, June 2010, http://www.richmondfed.org/publications/research/economic_brief/2010/pdf/eb_10-06.pdf.

[122] See, for example, Kenneth Scott and John Taylor, "How to Let Too Big to Fail Banks Fail," *Wall Street Journal*, May 16, 2013, p. A15; Hoover Institute, Resolution Project publications, available at http://www.hoover.org/taskforces/economic-policy/resolution-project/publications. For a comparison, see Sabrina Pellerin and John Walter, "Orderly Liquidation Authority as an Alternative to Bankruptcy," Federal Reserve Bank of Richmond, *Economic Quarterly*, vol. 98, no. 1, First Quarter 2012, p. 1.

[123] International Monetary Fund, "Resolution of Cross-Border Banks – A Proposed Framework for Enhanced Coordination," June 2010, available at http://www.imf.org/external/np/pp/eng/2010/061110.pdf.

Policy Response

In July 2008, Congress passed the Housing and Economic Recovery Act (HERA; P.L. 110-289), which included provisions creating a new regulator (the Federal Housing Finance Agency or FHFA) for the housing GSEs (the Federal Home Loan Banks, Fannie Mae, and Freddie Mac). The FHFA was given augmented powers to resolve the GSEs.[124] Under these powers, FHFA can manage assets, sign contracts, terminate claims, collect obligations, and perform management functions. In September 2008, Fannie Mae and Freddie Mac entered FHFA conservatorship, upon which FHFA took control of their operations while maintaining them as ongoing enterprises.[125] HERA also gave the Treasury Secretary unlimited authority to lend or invest in the GSEs through the end of 2009. This authority has been used to cover the GSEs' losses and prevent insolvency during conservatorship, and funds from Treasury continued to be transferred until 2012.[126] While existing shareholders saw their equity value plummet at the time of conservatorship, creditors and other counterparties have continued to be paid in full.

Title I of the Dodd-Frank Act (P.L. 111-203) requires systemically important firms (SIFIs) and BHCs with at least $50 billion in consolidated assets to periodically prepare resolution plans, also called "living wills," explaining how they could be resolved in a rapid and orderly manner. Failure to submit a credible resolution plan would trigger regulatory action. Title I also creates early remediation requirements for non-bank SIFIs that are in financial distress (banks already had early remediation requirements under existing statute).

Title II of the Dodd-Frank Act creates a resolution regime for financial firms whose failure would have "serious adverse effects on financial stability."[127] However, subsidiaries that are insurance companies would be resolved under state law, certain broker-dealers would be resolved by the Securities Investor Protection Corporation, and insured depository subsidiaries would be resolved under the FDIC's traditional resolution regime. The process for taking a firm into resolution has multiple steps and actors. First, a group of regulators (the group varies depending on the type of firm, but must always include the approval of two-thirds of the Federal Reserve's Board of Governors) must make a written recommendation to the Treasury Secretary that a firm should be resolved, explaining why bankruptcy would be inappropriate. Second, the Treasury Secretary must determine that resolution is necessary to avoid a default that would pose systemic risk to the financial system, and default cannot be prevented through a private sector alternative. Prior identification by the FSOC could be used as evidence that the firm's failure poses systemic risk, but it is not a necessary condition. Third, if the company disputes the Treasury Secretary's findings, it has limited rights to appeal in federal court. Finally, the FDIC manages the resolution.

The Dodd-Frank Act provides the FDIC with receivership powers, modeled on its bank receivership powers, with some differences, such as requirements that the FDIC consult with the primary regulator. As receiver, the FDIC can manage assets, sign contracts, terminate claims,

---

[124] For more information, see CRS Report RL34623, *Housing and Economic Recovery Act of 2008*, coordinated by N. Eric Weiss.

[125] For more information, see CRS Report RL34657, *Financial Institution Insolvency: Federal Authority over Fannie Mae, Freddie Mac, and Depository Institutions*, by David H. Carpenter and M. Maureen Murphy. Before HERA, Fannie Mae's and Freddie Mac's regulator had more limited powers of conservatorship and no powers of receivership.

[126] HERA required that the GSE be put into receivership if it became insolvent. Transfers from Treasury since 2008 to maintain solvency have had the effect of avoiding the receivership requirement.

[127] This finding does not require the firm to have been previously designated as systemically important for Title I's purposes of heightened prudential regulation.

collect obligations, and perform management functions. The Dodd-Frank Act sets priorities among classes of unsecured creditors, with senior executives and directors coming last before shareholders in order of priority. It requires that similarly situated creditors be treated similarly, unless doing so would increase the cost to the government. The FDIC is allowed to create bridge companies, as a way to divide good and bad assets, for a limited period of time to facilitate the resolution. Unlike FHFA's resolution regime, the Dodd-Frank regime does not allow for conservatorship.

The Dodd-Frank Act calls for shareholders and creditors to bear losses and management "responsible for the condition of the company" to be removed. The FDIC is allowed to use its funds to provide credit to the firm while in receivership if funding cannot be obtained from private credit markets. Unlike the resolution regime for banks, there is no least cost resolution requirement and the regime is not pre-funded (the FDIC may borrow from Treasury to finance it). Instead, costs that cannot be recouped in the process of resolution must be made up after the fact through assessments on counterparties (to the extent that their losses were smaller under receivership than they would have been in a traditional bankruptcy process) and risk-based assessments on financial firms with assets exceeding $50 billion. Since the rationale for limiting losses to counterparties is to prevent systemic risk, it is unclear how those counterparties could be assessed after the fact without also posing some systemic risk. A lack of pre-funding means that a firm's resolution will, in effect, be financed by its competitors (i.e., firms with assets exceeding $50 billion) instead of itself. The FDIC is limited to providing assistance in the resolution up to 10% of the failed firm's total consolidated assets in the first 30 days of the resolution; thereafter the limit becomes 90% of total consolidated assets available for repayment.

The FDIC has stated,

> the most promising resolution strategy [under Title II] from our point view will be to place the parent company into receivership and to pass its assets, principally investments in its subsidiaries, to a newly created bridge holding company. This will allow subsidiaries that are equity solvent and contribute to the franchise value of the firm to remain open and avoid the disruption that would likely accompany their closings ... .

> Equity claims of the firm's shareholders and the claims of the subordinated and unsecured debt holders will be left behind in the receivership....

> Therefore, initially, the bridge holding company will be owned by the receivership. The next stage in the resolution is to transfer ownership and control of the surviving franchise to private hands....

> The second step will be the conversion of the debt holders' claims to equity. The old debt holders of the failed parent will become the owners of the new company....[128]

This approach has been dubbed "Single Point of Entry," and the FDIC proposed a rule implementing it in December 2013.[129] A *BGOV* study argues that Single Point of Entry will only mitigate moral hazard if the holding company holds sufficient common equity and debt that can absorb losses in

---

[128] Martin J. Gruenberg, Acting Chairman of the Federal Deposit Insurance Corporation, Remarks to the Federal Reserve Bank of Chicago Bank Structure Conference; Chicago, IL, May 10, 2012.

[129] It can be accessed here: http://www.gpo.gov/fdsys/pkg/FR-2013-12-18/pdf/2013-30057.pdf. For more information on the FDIC as receiver under Title II, see http://www.fdic.gov/resauthority/.

resolution at the parent level; otherwise, investors will anticipate that public funds will be used to absorb losses.[130]

Selected Legislation in the 113th Congress

S.Amdt. 689 to the FY2014 budget resolution (S.Con.Res. 8) creates a non-binding budget reserve fund that allows for future legislation "related to any subsidies or funding advantage relative to other competitors received by bank holding companies with over $500 billion in total assets.... " It was adopted by the Senate on March 22, 2013.

H.Con.Res. 25, as amended and passed by the Senate on October 16, 2013, creates a non-binding budget reserve fund that allows for future legislation "related to any subsidies or funding advantage relative to other competitors received by bank holding companies with over $500 billion in total assets.... "

S. 2270, as passed the Senate on June 5, 2014, would allow regulators to exempt insurers from the "Collins Amendment" to the Dodd-Frank Act[131]—bank capital requirements that would otherwise apply because the insurers are bank holding companies or have been designated as systemically important. It also exempts such insurers from preparing financial statements according to Generally Accepted Accounting Principles (GAAP). Title I of H.R. 5461, which passed the House on September 16, 2014, contains the same language as S. 2270. It also includes three unrelated titles.

H.R. 4881, as ordered to be reported by the House Financial Services Committee on June 20, 2014, would place a one-year moratorium on FSOC designations of non-bank SIFIs upon enactment.

H.R. 5016, the Financial Services and General Government Appropriations Act, contained a provision introduced by H.Amdt. 1096 that

> None of the funds made available by this Act may be used to (1) designate any nonbank financial company as "too big to fail"; (2) designate any nonbank financial company as a "systemically important financial institution"; or (3) make a determination that material financial distress at a nonbank financial company, or the nature, scope, size, scale, concentration, interconnectedness, or mix of the activities of such company, could pose a threat to the financial stability of the United States.

It passed the House on July 16, 2014.

S. 798, the Terminating Bailouts for Taxpayer Fairness Act, would require a leverage ratio of at least 8% "equity capital" to "consolidated assets" for any bank or bank holding company with at least $50 billion of consolidated assets and a capital surcharge of at least 15% for any bank or bank holding company with at least $500 billion of consolidated assets. For other banks, it calls for leverage ratios comparable to leverage ratios in place as of May 1, 2013.[132] The leverage ratio

---

[130] Christopher Payne and Tony Costello, "Will Orderly Resolution Work?," *BGOV Analysis*, May 19, 2014.

[131] For background on the Collins Amendment, see the section above entitled "Regulating TBTF."

[132] The current Tier 1 leverage ratio is 4%. The bill provides a definition of equity and assets that make the quantitative ratios under the bill not directly comparable to ratios under current law, however.

for banks with at least $50 billion in assets and capital surcharge for banks with at least $500 billion in assets would apply to non-bank affiliates and subsidiaries, with the exception of subsidiaries or affiliates that are functionally regulated by the SEC or state insurance regulators. The bill would prevent "further implementation" of the Basel III agreement, which modifies safety and soundness regulation of small and large banks. The new capital requirements would supersede the ratios used under existing capital requirements that determine whether a bank is well-capitalized and the enhanced capital requirements in the Dodd-Frank Act for BHCs with at least $50 billion in assets and non-banks designated as systemically important (SIFIs). The bill allows, but does not require, regulators to establish risk-based capital requirements for financial institutions with at least $20 billion in assets if the regulators unanimously agree that the bill's other provisions are insufficient to prevent excessive risk concentration. The bill bans financial assistance to non-bank firms, subsidiaries, and affiliates from the federal government, Treasury's Exchange Stabilization Fund, the FDIC, or the Fed (through its discount window or Section 13(3) emergency powers). It also strikes from Section 806 of the Dodd-Frank Act access for financial market utilities (FMUs) to Federal Reserve account services, borrowing privileges, and interest payments. It also strikes the FDIC's systemic risk exception to least cost resolution under its bank resolution powers. The bill would modify the Federal Reserve's Small Bank Holding Company Policy Statement, which permits bank holding companies with consolidated assets of $500 million or less to acquire debt levels higher than permitted larger bank holding companies, by making the policy applicable to companies with assets of $5 billion or less. Under Dodd-Frank, bank holding companies subject to the Small Bank Holding Company Policy Statement are exempt from Basel III. The bill has other provisions, including exemptions from certain regulations for small or rural banks.

H.R. 3711/S. 1282, the 21st Century Glass-Steagall Act, would separate depository institutions from insurance companies, security entities, swap entities, and investment advisors. This legal separation includes banks affiliating with, owning, or having board members from such companies; operating in the same financial holding company; and holding an interest in a financial subsidiary. It would prohibit depository institutions from engaging in insurance activities, securities activities (including underwriting; market making; acting as a broker-dealer, futures commission merchant, investment adviser, or investment company; and making investments in hedge funds or private equity funds), swap activities (including acting as a swap dealer and major swap participant), agency transactional services, management consulting and counseling activities, proprietary trading, or prime brokerage activities. It would require banks to terminate non-bank affiliations, financial holding companies, and financial subsidiaries within five years, although federal bank regulators could require early termination or six-month extensions under certain circumstances. It would allow depository institutions to purchase securities on behalf of customers and for their own accounts, subject to restrictions. It would allow depository institutions to purchase swaps only to hedge a documented activity against specified risks. It would prohibit federal savings associations from investing in investment companies. The bill would also repeal provisions of the bankruptcy code that allow for qualified financial contracts, including repos, swaps, and master netting agreements, to avoid a stay or be liquidated, terminated, or accelerated.

S. 100, the Terminating the Expansion of Too Big to Fail Act, would repeal the provisions in the Dodd-Frank Act granting FSOC authority to designate non-bank SIFIs and Fed authority to subject them to enhanced prudential regulation, and all references to non-bank SIFIs in the Dodd-Frank Act. It would also repeal Title VIII of the Dodd-Frank Act, which provides for enhanced prudential supervision of payment, clearing, and settlement systems designated by FSOC as systemically important ("financial market utilities"). It has been referred to committee.

H.R. 1450/S. 685, Too Big to Fail, Too Big to Exist Act, would require the Secretary of the Treasury to produce a list of financial firms it believes are too big to fail, and break up those firms "so that their failure would no longer cause a catastrophic effect on the United States.... " It has been referred to committee.

H.R. 129/S. 985 Return to Prudent Banking Act, would prohibit affiliations between depositories and investment banks or securities firms. It has been referred to committee.

H.R. 613, Systemic Risk Mitigation Act, would require BHCs with at least $50 billion in assets to issue long-term subordinated debt equal to at least 15% of the bank's assets. If the average daily closing price of a credit default swap using the subordinated debt as a reference entity exceeds 0.5 percentage points, the Fed would require the BHC to increase its Tier 1 capital. If the closing price exceeds 0.75 percentage points, the Fed may suspend the BHC's dividend payments. If the closing price exceeds 1 percentage point, the company would be placed into receivership under the Orderly Liquidation Authority. The bill repeals the Fed's authority to implement enhanced prudential regulation of banks with $50 billion or more in assets and non-bank SIFIs designated by FSOC. It also repeals the Volcker Rule ban on proprietary trading and hedge fund sponsorship. The bill was referred to committee.

H.R. 2266, Subsidy Reserve Act, would require the Fed to estimate the implicit subsidy enjoyed by BHCs with more than $500 billion in assets and non-banks designated as SIFIs by the FSOC, and would require those firms to set aside that amount in a "subsidy reserve" account.

H.R. 4060, Systemic Risk Designation Improvement Act, would require FSOC to designate BHCs as SIFIs through the same process used to designate non-banks as SIFIs beginning one year after enactment. It would prohibit FSOC from designating any BHC with less than $50 billion in assets. It would repeal the section of the Dodd-Frank Act that subjects all BHCs with more than $50 billion in assets to enhanced supervision. H.R. 3036 is a similar bill.

H.R. 4532 would change the mandatory threshold for enhanced Fed supervision for banks from $50 billion to $250 billion in assets. For banks with total assets between $50 billion and $250 billion, FSOC would be required to determine that the bank posed systemic risk in order for the bank to be subject to enhanced supervision. Other provisions of the Dodd-Frank Act applying to banks with more than $50 billion in assets are also modified to apply only to banks that are subject to enhanced supervision.

Representative Dave Camp's Tax Reform Act of 2014 discussion draft includes an excise tax of 0.035% on bank and non-bank SIFIs levied on the SIFI's total consolidated assets (as reported to the Federal Reserve) in excess of $500 billion.[133]

Conclusion

Contagion stemming from problems at TBTF (or too interconnected to fail) firms is widely regarded to have been one of the primary sources of systemic risk during the recent financial crisis. To avoid contagion, a series of ad hoc government interventions were undertaken that

---

[133] The discussion draft is posted here: http://waysandmeans.house.gov/uploadedfiles/ statutory_text_tax_reform_act_of_2014_discussion_draft__022614.pdf.

protected creditors and counterparties—in a few cases, also managers and shareholders—of large and interconnected firms from losses. Economic theory suggests that these interventions exacerbated the moral hazard implications of TBTF, reducing the incentive for creditors and counterparties to safeguard against extreme outcomes, and increased the incentive to become larger and more interconnected going forward. Competing theories blame the lack of regulatory authority and failed regulation for the role of TBTF in the recent crisis. The failures of both highly regulated banks and lightly regulated non-banks suggest that neither lack of regulation nor failed regulation were solely responsible for TBTF.

Policy before the financial crisis could be characterized as an implicit market discipline approach with ambiguity about which firms policy makers considered to be TBTF and how the imminent failure of a systemically important firm might be addressed. This ambiguity was defended on the grounds that it would result in less moral hazard than if TBTF firms were explicitly identified, since the ambiguity would promote market discipline. As the crisis unfolded, policy quickly shifted to an implicit government assistance approach where Bear Stearns, Fannie Mae, Freddie Mac, and AIG received direct government support and several emergency programs were instituted to ensure that other financial firms remained liquid and solvent. Not every large failing firm received assistance, however, with Lehman Brothers being the notable exception. Both before and during the crisis, policy could be characterized as ad hoc because arguably no general approach or principles were articulated that clearly signaled to firms or investors how a systemically important firm could expect to be treated in different scenarios. Some believe that this policy uncertainty made the crisis worse.

The rapid shift from market discipline to government assistance during the crisis undermines the future credibility of the pre-crisis policy approach. If policy makers wanted to return to a market discipline approach, making that approach effective would arguably require statutory changes that bolster policy makers' credibility by "tying their hands" to make assistance more difficult in the event of a future TBTF failure. This could be accomplished by eliminating broad, open-ended authority that was invoked during the last crisis, such as Section 13(3) of the Federal Reserve Act and the FDIC's systemic risk exception to least cost resolution. Policy makers cannot be prevented from enacting future legislation allowing assistance, however, much as TARP was enacted expeditiously when the crisis worsened in September 2008. If investors do not believe that market discipline will be maintained because policy makers face short-term incentives to provide government assistance in times of crisis, then a "no bailouts" promise would not prevent moral hazard.

One view is that the genie cannot be put back in the bottle—market participants now believe that the government will provide assistance to TBTF firms based on the 2008 experience, in which case they face little incentive to monitor or respond to excessive risk taking. If so, the policy options to mitigate moral hazard are to regulate TBTF firms or use government policy to reduce the systemic risk posed by TBTF firms.

In theory, a special regulatory regime for TBTF firms could set safety and soundness standards at a strict enough level to neutralize moral hazard effects. The complexity and interconnectedness of large firms complicates their effective regulation, however. Moreover, a special regulatory regime for TBTF firms could backfire if regulatory capture occurs. Special regulation makes explicit which firms are TBTF, removing any ambiguity that might promote market discipline. As market discipline wanes, the burden on regulators to mitigate moral hazard increases. If regulators are unwilling or unable to apply regulatory standards that negate the benefits of being TBTF, then being subject to the special regulatory regime could give TBTF firms a competitive advantage over their industry rivals. The experience of Fannie Mae and Freddie Mac points to the dangers of this approach. Those two firms were subject to their own regulatory regime prior to the crisis and were able to borrow at lower interest rates than other financial firms, presumably because of the implicit government guarantee of their obligations.

Systemic risk stemming from TBTF can also be mitigated by reducing potential spillover and contagion effects. Examples of proposals to reduce contagion effects include a special resolution regime for failing systemically important firms and placing limits on counterparty exposure to large firms. Events in 2008, however, demonstrate the challenge in eliminating systemic risk posed by TBTF firms because it is unlikely that policy makers will correctly anticipate all of the channels of contagion in a crisis. Moreover, in determining whether to use government resources to limit losses to creditors, the receiver faces the same short-term incentives to spare creditors from losses that lead to moral hazard. Critics point to the open-ended assistance to Fannie Mae and Freddie Mac since 2008 as a cautionary tale, although this was through government conservatorship, rather than receivership.

Some argue for eliminating TBTF directly by reducing the size or scope of the largest firms. It is uncertain what size limit would eliminate TBTF—given that interconnectedness is a nebulous concept—and success can only be confirmed by observing what occurs after a firm fails. Weighed against the benefits of eliminating the TBTF problem, the benefits to the financial system that would be lost by eliminating large firms are also disputed. In the case of reducing scope, some large firms would remain, and they would be less diversified against risk. Fannie Mae and Freddie Mac are examples of large, narrowly focused firms that many nonetheless viewed as TBTF.

A comprehensive policy is likely to incorporate more than one approach because different approaches are aimed at different parts of the problem. Some approaches focus on preventive measures (keeping TBTF firms out of trouble), whereas others are reactive (addressing what to do in the event of a TBTF failure). Some policy approaches are complementary—others could undermine each other. A market discipline approach is arguably most likely to succeed if coupled with size limits—although size limits thwart market-based profit incentives and outcomes. Policies that involve identification of TBTF firms, such as a special regulatory regime, are less compatible with a market discipline approach. Efforts to minimize spillover effects could be more effective if the TBTF firms are regulated for safety and soundness, so that spillover effects can more easily be identified ahead of time. Policy makers have historically coped with the moral hazard associated with deposit insurance through a combination of safety and soundness regulation, a resolution regime, and limits on spillover effects (e.g., limits on counterparty exposure). (Market discipline's role is limited by deposit insurance, but it plays a role with uninsured depositors and other creditors.) Yet TBTF poses some additional challenges to the bank regulation model, such as the difficulties of imposing a strict least cost resolution requirement on a resolution regime and effectively regulating firms with complex and wide-ranging activities.

Each of these policy approaches to coping with TBTF has strengths and weaknesses; there is no silver-bullet solution to the problem because future policy makers face incentives to deviate from the approach to avoid crises, please interest groups, increase financial innovation and the availability of credit, and so on. Judging the relative merits of each policy approach depends in part on which approach future policy makers can best commit to and effectively carry out.

The Dodd-Frank Act devised a strategy to end TBTF that, to varying degrees, incorporated each approach discussed in this report. Ultimately, the only definitive test of whether the strategy succeeds is whether the failure of a large firm can be managed without a "bailout" and whether large firms stay healthy in a financial downturn—events that may not occur for years or even decades. Until then, perceptions of whether the TBTF problem still exists may develop (and be observable in market data), which could subsequently be proven true or false.

Although TBTF was one cause of systemic risk in the recent crisis, it was not the only one. The Dodd-Frank Act also attempted to address other sources of systemic risk. Although the broader issue of systemic risk is beyond the scope of this report, some policy options discussed in this report may be more effective at mitigating systemic risk if applied more broadly than to TBTF firms exclusively. Otherwise, some sources of systemic risk may migrate to firms not regulated for safety and soundness, without increasing the stability of the overall financial system. If systemic risk mainly stems from certain activities, regardless of size, a policy focus on large institutions could risk creating a false sense of security.

Risk is central to financial activity, so an optimal system is probably not one where large firms never fail. An optimal system is one in which a large firm can fail without destabilizing the financial system. The only system that can guarantee that large firms will not cause systemic risk is one without large firms, but a system without large firms may be less efficient. Other approaches seek to limit systemic risk to acceptable levels. Creating a more stable financial system by mitigating the moral hazard associated with TBTF may result in credit becoming more expensive and less available in the short run, but the availability of credit could be less volatile over time. Some policy makers would consider a tradeoff of less credit for a more stable financial system to be a tradeoff worth taking, considering that the recent crisis resulted in the deepest and longest recession since the Great Depression. Arguably, part of the cause of the crisis was that credit became too readily available, at least in some sectors (e.g., the housing bubble). At least partly offsetting the higher costs of capital for firms designated as systemically important would be relatively lower costs of capital for other firms.

Appendix. Selected Historical Experiences With "Too Big To Fail"

Before the Recent Crisis

There have always been large financial firms in the United States, but concentration within the banking sector and non-bank financial sector has increased in recent decades. This growth is a reflection of both policy changes that made growth easier and market changes that made growth more profitable. For example, technological change altered the types of financial products that could be offered and the relative costs of offering them, and investments in information technology may be subject to economies of scale.

Two important policy changes that allowed financial firms to become larger since the Great Depression were the erosion of the separation of banking from other financial services (such as investment banking) and the erosion of prohibitions on interstate banking.

The Glass-Steagall Act forbade commercial banks from underwriting or trading in certain types of securities and affiliating with a business engaged principally in investment banking. It forbade investment banks from accepting deposits and forbade the same company from owning a commercial bank and an investment bank. The Bank Holding Company Act prohibited banks from affiliating with companies engaging in insurance underwriting and defined the activities closely related to banking that banks were allowed to engage in.[134] Implementation of these restrictions relied upon regulators' judgment and interpretation, which evolved over time. Regulators interpreted which securities commercial banks were eligible to purchase, which activities fell within the "business of banking," and how closely affiliated commercial banks could be with investment banks. From the 1970s on, regulators began to interpret Glass-Steagall more loosely, and differences between commercial banks and investment banks began to erode.[135]

The Gramm-Leach-Bliley Act (GLBA) of 1999 repealed the prohibition on affiliations between commercial banks and investment banks or insurance companies, and created a financial holding company (FHC) structure to facilitate those affiliations. Within a FHC or BHC, firewalls are required to prevent financial problems at non-depository subsidiary from affecting a depository subsidiary. (GLBA kept intact the provisions of Glass-Steagall preventing investment banks from accepting deposits.) While GLBA made it easier for firms in diverse lines of business to operate under a holding company structure, it also formalized Federal Reserve supervision and regulation of complex financial firms. GLBA formalized the Fed's role as "umbrella regulator" of bank holding companies and financial holding companies and the Office of Thrift Supervision as umbrella regulator of thrift holding companies, and allowed the regulators to set consolidated capital standards at the holding company level. The Fed's role as umbrella regulator gave it very limited powers, however, to regulate or examine subsidiaries that already had a functional regulator, such as investment firms and insurers.[136]

---

[134] 70 Stat. 133.

[135] For more information on the erosion of Glass Steagall, see CRS Report R41181, *Permissible Securities Activities of Commercial Banks Under the Glass-Steagall Act (GSA) and the Gramm-Leach-Bliley Act (GLBA)*, by David H. Carpenter and M. Maureen Murphy.

[136] For more information, see Mark Greenlee, "Historical Review of 'Umbrella Regulation' by the Board of Governors (continued...)

Traditionally, banks were chartered to operate in one state. Interstate banking by national banks was allowed with a state's consent under the McFadden Act of 1927 (P.L. 69-639). The absence of state consent prevented widespread interstate banking for the next several decades, curbing the growth in nationwide banks. A series of legislative and regulatory changes led to the spread of interstate banking in the 1980s and 1990s. The Riegle-Neal Interstate Banking and Branching Efficiency Act of 1994 (P.L. 103-328) further liberalized interstate banking.[137] The Riegle-Neal Act prevented mergers resulting in a BHC exceeding 10% of national deposits and 30% of a state's deposits.

The history of government bailouts on TBTF grounds before 2008 is largely limited to the cases of a few banks. In cases where government intervention to prevent the failure of non-banks on TBTF grounds was urged (Long-Term Capital Management), the government ultimately decided not to intervene financially to save the companies, and the spillover effects were limited. The **Appendix** does not review cases where federal assistance was provided on other than systemic risk grounds. Most of the economic arguments of how financial firms are prone to contagion and runs do not apply to non-financial firms. Examples include assistance to non-financial firms such as Lockheed in 1970, Chrysler in 1980, and Chrysler and GM in 2008, where assistance was justified on the grounds of avoiding negative effects on the region or industry.[138]

Resolution of Banks Before and After the Federal Deposit Insurance Corporation Improvement Act

Currently, the two main methods for resolving failed banks are "depositor payoff" (winding down the bank and paying off depositors) and "purchase and assumption" (selling parts of failed banks, such as deposits and sound assets, to healthy banks).[139] In either method, uninsured depositors and creditors are compensated according to the priority of their claims to the extent that the proceeds of the sale or liquidation allow; only insured depositors are guaranteed to be fully compensated. In practice, it was standard for the acquiring bank to take on the accounts of the uninsured depositors in the case of a purchase and assumption, resulting in no losses for the latter.[140] According to Stern and Feldman, "Reliance on [purchase and assumption] led the deposit insurer to cover all depositors. The FDIC covered more than 99 percent of uninsured depositors from 1985 to 1991, a period in which roughly 1,200 commercial banks failed."[141]

(...continued)

of the Federal Reserve System," Federal Reserve Bank of Cleveland, working paper 08-07, October 2008.

[137] For more information, see CRS Report 94-744, *The Riegle-Neal Interstate Banking and Branching Efficiency Act of 1994*, by M. Maureen Murphy. (This report is out of print, but available by request.)

[138] See General Accounting Office, *Guidelines for Rescuing Large Failing Firms and Municipalities*, GAO Report GGD-84-34, March 29, 1984; CRS Report R41401, *General Motors' Initial Public Offering: Review of Issues and Implications for TARP*, by Bill Canis, Baird Webel, and Gary Shorter; CRS Report R41940, *TARP Assistance for Chrysler: Restructuring and Repayment Issues*, by Baird Webel and Bill Canis.

[139] For more information on the resolution process, see CRS Report RL34657, *Financial Institution Insolvency: Federal Authority over Fannie Mae, Freddie Mac, and Depository Institutions*, by David H. Carpenter and M. Maureen Murphy.

[140] Federal Deposit Insurance Corporation, *Managing The Crisis*, Part 1, Chapter 3, August 1998, http://www.fdic.gov/bank/historical/managing/history1-03.pdf.

[141] Gary Stern and Ron Feldman, *Too Big to Fail*, (Washington, D.C.: Brookings Institution Press), 2004, p. 151.

In the past, an alternative option for resolving troubled banks was open bank assistance. Under open bank assistance, the FDIC could make loans to banks that could no longer obtain funding from the private sector in order to keep banks operating as an ongoing concern as an alternative to resolving them. Banks receiving open bank assistance were often required by the FDIC to replace management and dilute shareholders, but creditors and depositors would be unaffected. In 1950, Congress granted the FDIC the ability to give open bank assistance to troubled banks if the bank's "continued existence was determined to be 'essential' to providing adequate banking services in the community," leaving the determination of "essential" to the FDIC.[142] "Essentiality" was invoked 10 times between 1971 and 1991, the largest example of which was for Continental Illinois, which is discussed below in detail.[143] In 1982, the Garn-St. Germain Act broadened the FDIC's ability to provide open bank assistance to include cases where the FDIC determined that it would cost less than liquidation.

Open bank assistance was not used until the 1970s, and was not used frequently until the Savings and Loan Crisis in the 1980s. Between 1980 and 1992, it was used for 133 banks, which were larger on average than banks resolved under the other methods. 70 of the 133 instances were for banks within two specific bank holding companies, BancTexas and First City Bancorporation of Texas. While these two were not among the largest banks in the country, the FDIC provided them with open bank assistance on the grounds that their failure would lead to contagion throughout Texas banks, which had been weakened by the energy bust.[144]

Open bank assistance could be used because a bank was deemed TBTF, but it could also be used for other reasons, including regional difficulties, which were more acute before interstate banking. Some of the banks to which it was applied were large by state standards, but were not particularly large at a national level (which few banks were, at the time). Furthermore, prior to various legislation in the 1980s, the purchase and assumption method was relatively more costly and often resulted in litigation, making open bank assistance relatively more attractive from regulators' perspective. Thus, it is difficult to establish how many of these 133 cases were motivated by TBTF concerns, or how much this experience had led banks, creditors, and counterparties to conclude that large banks would not be allowed to fail.

Regulators could also avoid resolving a bank through regulatory forbearance. An example of regulatory forbearance is allowing banks to temporarily operate with capital below required levels. Regulators could choose to allow regulatory forbearance on TBTF grounds, although in practice, it often occurred with small thrifts in the 1980s.[145]

Many economists criticized the handling of bank resolutions in the 1980s, arguing that regulatory forbearance worsened the moral hazard problem, because a troubled bank allowed to remain in operation had even more incentive to take risks. Legislation in 1991 reduced the potential for regulatory forbearance by requiring prompt corrective action and least cost resolution of troubled

---

[142] Federal Deposit Insurance Corporation, *Managing The Crisis*, Part 1, Chapter 5, August 1998, p. 153, http://www.fdic.gov/bank/historical/managing/history1-05.pdf.

[143] Federal Deposit Insurance Corporation, "Continental Illinois and 'Too Big to Fail'," *History of the Eighties*, Ch. 7, http://www.fdic.gov/bank/historical/history/235_258.pdf.

[144] Besides FDIC resolutions, there were a large number of thrift resolutions in the 1980s. Since these institutions tended to be small, this experience is not central to the TBTF issue.

[145] FDIC, "The Savings and Loan Crisis and Its Relationship to Banking," *History of the Eighties – Lessons for the Future*, December 1997, Ch. 4, http://www.fdic.gov/bank/historical/history/.

banks.[146] These legislative changes and others made open bank assistance less likely, and according to FDIC data, open bank assistance was not used between 1993 and 2008.[147] (Purchase and assumption continued to be the main method of resolution after 1991, but bids involving only insured deposits became more common.) Current law, as amended by the 1991 legislation, allows the FDIC to waive the least cost resolution method if the Treasury Secretary (in consultation with the President, Federal Reserve, and FDIC) believes that least cost resolution would cause systemic risk, however.[148] TBTF is potential grounds for invoking this systemic risk exception. Thus, while the 1991 legislation is perceived to have reduced moral hazard at small banks, it is not clear whether it had a significant effect on the TBTF problem.

Penn Central Railroad

After unsuccessfully seeking financial assistance from Congress and the Fed, Penn Central Railroad filed for bankruptcy in June 1970. At that time, it had $82 million in commercial paper outstanding, and when it filed for bankruptcy, the Fed feared its bankruptcy would cause disruption in the commercial paper market for all borrowers. The Fed temporarily removed legal interest rate ceilings to avoid a credit crunch and "made clear that the Federal Reserve discount window would be available to assist banks in meeting the needs of businesses unable to roll over maturing commercial paper."[149] In other words, the Fed was willing to assist the counterparties to prevent contagion from a perceived TBTF failure, rather than preventing the firm from failing. In any case, the perceived contagion from that source did not materialize—data do not indicate an unusual amount of discount window lending by the Fed in 1970.[150]

Beginning in 1974, the federal government provided financial assistance to maintain the viability of passenger rail service in the wake of Penn Central's bankruptcy. This assistance was not provided to prevent bankruptcy or to maintain financial stability, and is therefore beyond the scope of this report.

Franklin National

Franklin National, the nation's 20th-largest bank, experienced financial difficulties in 1974. Fearing that its failure would destabilize money markets, the Fed purchased its foreign exchange balances and futures contracts and provided it loans through the discount window to keep it afloat. When Franklin was resolved later that year, the FDIC assumed Franklin's $1.7 billion unpaid discount window loan.[151]

---

[146] The Federal Deposit Insurance Corporation Improvement Act, P.L. 102-242. Previously, the FDIC had to demonstrate that its resolution method was less costly than an insured deposit payoff; that requirement could be waived in the case of the "essentiality" exception noted above.

[147] FDIC data on bank failures can be accessed at http://www2 fdic.gov/hsob/SelectRpt.asp?EntryTyp=30.

[148] 12 U.S.C 1823(c).

[149] Federal Reserve annual report quoted in Anna Schwartz, "The Misuse of the Fed's Discount Window," *Federal Reserve Bank of St. Louis Review*, September/October 1992, p. 58.

[150] For more information on the Fed's response to the Penn Central failure, see Mark Carlson and David Wheelock, "The Lender of Last Resort: Lessons from the Fed's First 100 Years," Federal Reserve Bank of St. Louis, working paper 2012-056B, February 2013.

[151] Mark Carlson and David Wheelock, "The Lender of Last Resort: Lessons from the Fed's First 100 Years," Federal Reserve Bank of St. Louis, Working Paper 2012-056B, February 2013.

Continental Illinois

Continental Illinois was the nation's seventh-largest bank in 1984.[152] Continental Illinois losses have been tied to its aggressive growth in commercial lending beginning in the late 1970s.[153] Continental Illinois' problems began in 1982 with the failure of a correspondent bank, and came to a head in 1984 with a run by some uninsured depositors. Despite being subject to the FDIC's resolution regime, the Comptroller of the Currency at the time testified that Continental Illinois could not be allowed to fail because it would have caused the failure of more than 100 banks with deposits at Continental Illinois, and dozens of corporate customers.[154] It began receiving federal assistance in 1984 in the form of discount window loans from the Fed that peaked at $8 billion and a guarantee by the FDIC of all uninsured depositors and creditors. Eventually, policy makers decided a more permanent solution was needed. Instead of taking Continental Illinois into receivership, the FDIC purchased $3.5 billion of problem loans and $1 billion of preferred shares, and repaid $3.5 billion in loans from the Federal Reserve. The final cost to FDIC was $1.1 billion.[155] The chairman of the board and chief executive officer were replaced, and the FDIC received an option to acquire Continental Illinois' stock to cover potential losses.

Continental Illinois was regulated for safety and soundness, operating in an era before many financial regulations were liberalized by the Gramm-Leach-Bliley Act and other legislative and regulatory changes.[156] One problem identified was the pace with which regulators addressed Continental's problems—the bank failed in September; the previous May, OCC had stated that the bank's capital ratios "compared favorably to those of other multinational banks."[157] Had regulators addressed Continental Illinois' financial problems sooner, the ultimate cost to taxpayers may have been lower. Continental Illinois also led to a more explicit TBTF policy, at least for banks. At a congressional hearing, Comptroller of the Currency Todd Conover testified that "the federal government won't currently allow any of the nation's 11 largest banks to fail," but did not name those banks.[158] One study found that after this testimony, the 11 largest banks received higher ratings on their bonds and borrowed at lower costs.[159]

Long-Term Capital Management

In 1998, the hedge fund Long-Term Capital Management (LTCM) experienced a liquidity crisis as a result of large leveraged trading losses resulting from an unanticipated widening of credit

---

[152] Federal Deposit Insurance Corporation, "Continental Illinois National Bank and Trust Company," *Managing The Crisis*, Part 2, Chapter 4, August 1998, http://www.fdic.gov/bank/historical/managing/history2-04.pdf.

[153] Federal Deposit Insurance Corporation, "Continental Illinois and 'Too Big to Fail'," *History of the Eighties*, ch. 7, http://www.fdic.gov/bank/historical/history/235_258.pdf.

[154] The claim that more than 100 banks would have failed has been disputed in Larry Wall, "Too Big to Fail After FDICIA," *Federal Reserve Bank of Atlanta Economic Review*, no. 78, January/February 1993, p. 1.

[155] Federal Deposit Insurance Corporation, "Continental Illinois National Bank and Trust Company," *Managing The Crisis*, Part 2, Chapter 4, August 1998, http://www.fdic.gov/bank/historical/managing/history2-04.pdf.

[156] The role of regulatory supervision in Continental Illinois' failure is discussed in Federal Deposit Insurance Corporation, "Continental Illinois and 'Too Big to Fail'," *History of the Eighties*, Ch. 7, http://www.fdic.gov/bank/historical/history/235_258.pdf.

[157] Office of the Comptroller of the Currency, "Statement on Continental Illinois," news release 84-45, May 10, 1984.

[158] Tim Carrington, "U.S. Won't Let 11 Biggest Banks in Nation Fail," *Wall Street Journal*, September 20, 1984, p. 1.

[159] Donald Morgan and Kevin Stiroh, *Too Big to Fail After All These Years*, Federal Reserve Bank of New York, Staff Report Number 220, New York, NY, September 2005.

---

spreads. To avoid a failure that the Fed thought could be destabilizing to the financial system as a whole, the New York Fed organized a group of large financial institutions to offer LTCM private assistance in the form of a $3.6 billion capital injection, without the use of any public funds or guarantees. The Fed was concerned that liquidating LTCM's large trading positions could destabilize financial markets and impose large losses on counterparties. In the weeks before the capital injection, LTCM's capital had been rapidly depleted by losses, but its net asset value was still positive, albeit small, at the time of the intervention.[160] The Fed's actions in this case could be described as helping the rescuing firms (who were also LTCM counterparties) to overcome the collective action problem—the firms involved were better off recapitalizing the firm than liquidating it, but unless they could act collectively, it was in no firm's individual interest to recapitalize it alone. Critics claimed the Fed's intervention was unnecessary, as an alternative offer from another group of investors to purchase the firm on less attractive terms was also made.[161]

As in 2007, overall markets came under unusual stress and became illiquid in 1998. Unlike 2007, the stress passed and markets recovered quickly in 1998. Although it is unknown what would have happened had LTCM been allowed to fail, this experience seemed at the time to provide a framework for coping with problems at a TBTF firm—preventing LTCM's failure prevented contagion from spreading to other institutions or markets, and conditions were able to quickly normalize. Since the government did not offer financial assistance, it could continue to claim that TBTF firms would not be bailed out. LTCM's problems did not cause investors to doubt the health of similar firms, as happened in the recent crisis. A lesson that many drew from this episode was that market mechanisms and existing policy tools could contain the contagion effects resulting from liquidity problems at a highly leveraged and interconnected firm that was not regulated for safety and soundness.

Firms in 2008

Several large firms experienced difficulty in 2008, and these problems were resolved in a number of ways. Bear Stearns and AIG were rescued from failure through government assistance. Lehman Brothers filed for bankruptcy. Fannie Mae and Freddie Mac entered government conservatorship. Wachovia and Washington Mutual were acquired by other banks without government assistance.

As the name implies, "too big to fail" requires both size and the prospect of failure. Part of the reason the policy issue came to the forefront in 2008 and not earlier is because the crisis led to so many failures of large and small firms. The probability of a large (or small) firm failing in 2008 was much higher than in the decades of financial stability leading up to 2008. More contentious is the argument made by some that the probability of failure was also higher in 2008 because large firms were taking greater risks than in previous decades. Evidence presented in support of this argument includes the rise over time in financial firms' use of leverage (debt-to-equity ratios),[162]

---

[160] For more details, see U.S. General Accounting Office, *Long-Term Capital Management*, GGD-00-3, October 1999, http://www.gao.gov/archive/2000/gg00003.pdf.

[161] Kevin Dowd, *Too Big to Fail? Long-Term Capital Management and the Federal Reserve*, Cato Institute, Briefing Paper Number 52, Washington, DC, September 1999, http://www.cato.org/pubs/briefs/bp52.pdf.

[162] The increase in leverage was more pronounced at investment banks than commercial banks. See, for example Sebnem Kalemli-Ozcan, Bent Sorensen, Sevcan Yesiltas, "Leverage Across Firms, Banks, and Countries," working paper, August 2011.

unstable sources of liquidity, and complex financial instruments such as credit default swaps (which could be used by a firm to reduce or increase certain forms of risk).

Bear Stearns

In the recent crisis, the investment bank Bear Stearns was the first TBTF firm to receive government assistance to avert failure.[163] Bear Stearns was not a bank holding company regulated for safety and soundness, nor subject to the FDIC's resolution regime.[164] It came under severe liquidity pressures in early March 2008, when creditors refused to roll over short-term debt and counterparties withdrew funds, in what observers have coined a non-bank run. An SEC press release a few days before its takeover indicated that Bear Stearns had $17 billion of cash and other liquid assets—an amount that was quickly depleted by the run.[165] The run was set off by concerns that Bear Stearns held a large portfolio of illiquid, "troubled" assets that investors believed would continue losing value in the future and deplete its remaining capital.

By the weekend of March 15, it had become clear that Bear Stearns could not survive the run by creditors. Although Bear Stearns was not indisputably "too big to fail" (it was the 138[th-]largest firm by revenues in 2007 on *Fortune Magazine*'s Fortune 500 list),[166] some policy makers argued for government intervention on the grounds that Bear Stearns was "too interconnected to fail," meaning too many counterparties and markets would be disrupted by a traditional bankruptcy filing.[167] The Fed sought a healthy firm to acquire Bear Stearns, but was unable to find a willing partner without financial assistance. Over the weekend of March 15, the Fed arranged and assisted in the takeover of Bear Stearns by J.P. Morgan Chase at a very low purchase price (originally $2 per share, subsequently increased to $10 per share), which Bear Stearns' board of directors agreed to accept instead of pursuing a bankruptcy filing. The takeover led to replacement of some of Bear Stearns' management and the low share price meant that shareholders were effectively diluted, although they likely fared better than they would have in a bankruptcy proceeding. J.P. Morgan Chase agreed to honor all of Bear Stearns' contractual obligations, however, which meant that creditors and counterparties were fully compensated, creating moral hazard problems.

The main stumbling block for J.P. Morgan Chase was Bear Stearns' large portfolio of troubled assets. As part of the agreement, the Fed agreed to purchase up to $30 billion of Bear Stearns' assets through Maiden Lane I, a new Limited Liability Corporation (LLC) based in Delaware that it created and controlled. J.P. Morgan Chase would bear up to $1.15 billion in future first losses, based on assets valued at $29.97 billion at marked-to-market prices by Bear Stearns on March 14, 2008.[168] About half of these assets were collateralized mortgage obligations. The Fed has

---

[163] For more detailed information, see CRS Report RL34427, *Financial Turmoil: Federal Reserve Policy Responses*, by Marc Labonte.

[164] Bear Stearns complied with an SEC net capital rule, but was not subject to safety and soundness supervision. For more information, see CRS Report R43087, *Who Regulates Whom and How? An Overview of U.S. Financial Regulatory Policy for Banking and Securities Markets*, by Edward V. Murphy.

[165] Securities and Exchange Commission, "Statement of SEC Division of Trading and Markets Regarding The Bear Stearns Companies," press release 2008-44, March 11, 2008, http://www.sec.gov/news/press/2008/2008-44.htm.

[166] List can be accessed at http://money.cnn.com/magazines/fortune/fortune500/2007/full_list/index.html.

[167] Greg Ip, "Central Bank Offers Loans to Brokers, Cuts Key Rate," *Wall Street Journal*, March 17, 2008, p. A1.

[168] Federal Reserve Bank of New York, "New York Fed Completes Financing Arrangement Related to JPMorgan Chase's Acquisition of Bear Stearns," press release, June 26, 2008.

gradually sold off the assets, in order "to minimize disruption to financial markets and maximize recovery value."[169] This transaction exposed the Fed to significant credit risk on its balance sheet for the first time in decades. By 2012, Maiden Lane had received more from asset sales than the Fed had contributed to their purchases. Principal and interest were recouped, and some assets remained that could provide the Fed with additional future profits when sold. CBO estimated at the time of inception that the Maiden Lane transaction was not subsidized since the assets were bought at market prices.[170] In addition, during the JP Morgan Chase takeover, Bear Stearns had an average of $13.9 billion loans outstanding from the Primary Dealer Credit Facility from March 17 to June 23, 2008, and $1.5 billion loans outstanding from the Term Securities Lending Facility from March 28 to May 9, 2008.[171] These facilities were broadly based emergency Fed programs created during the crisis. These loans were repaid in full with interest.

Had Bear Stearns been a bank holding company, it might have been able to boost its liquidity with collateralized loans from the Fed. It also would have been subject to prudential regulation by the Fed that might have required it to pursue a more conservative business strategy. Since it was not a bank holding company, the Fed relied on emergency lending powers not used to lend to non-banks since the Great Depression. Since these powers limited the Fed to lending, the Fed was required to set up the LLC structure to make the asset purchases possible.

Although Bear Stearns' liquidity problems were driving it into bankruptcy had the government not interceded, it is unclear whether it was insolvent. Before that weekend, Bear Stearns was not insolvent by two common measurements: its stock price (representing the current market valuation of the firm's net worth) was still $30 per share, and its primary regulator, the Securities and Exchange Commission (SEC), issued a press release on March 11 that stated that Bear Stearns was adequately capitalized according to its net capital rule.[172] Even after the crisis, existing shares were valued positively in the J.P. Morgan Chase takeover, and no capital was provided to Bear Stearns as part of the Fed's assistance (since the assets bought by Maiden Lane were purchased at market value, according to the Fed). On the other hand, J.P. Morgan stated that the equity in Bear Stearns was exhausted and J.P. Morgan Chase took additional losses from costs associated with the Bear Stearns acquisition.[173]

Unlike the LTCM experience, the rescue of Bear Stearns arguably did not cause investors to conclude that Bear Stearns was an isolated "bad apple." Instead, speculation persisted over the next few months that other investment banks would suffer the same fate—speculation that came to a head with the wave of financial firm failures in September 2008.

---

[169] Federal Reserve Bank of New York, "Statement on Financing Arrangement of JPMorgan Chase's Acquisition of Bear Stearns," press release, March 24, 2008.

[170] Congressional Budget Office, *The Budgetary Impact and Subsidy Costs of the Federal Reserve's Actions During the Financial Crisis*, May 2010.

[171] Lending records can be accessed at http://www.federalreserve.gov/newsevents/reform_pdcf.htm.

[172] Securities and Exchange Commission, "Statement of SEC Division of Trading and Markets Regarding The Bear Stearns Companies," press release 2008-44, March 11, 2008, http://www.sec.gov/news/press/2008/2008-44.htm.

[173] J.P. Morgan Chase, Annual Report, 2008, p. 9, http://files.shareholder.com/downloads/ONE/2506919982x0x283416/66cc70ba-5410-43c4-b20b-181974bc6be6/2008_AR_Complete_AR.pdf.

Ban on Naked Short Selling in July 2008

As financial turmoil worsened in the summer of 2008, the stock value of many large financial firms fell quickly. The SEC responded on July 15, 2008, by announcing that investors would no longer be able to "naked short sell" the stocks of 19 large financial firms, an investment strategy that would pay off if the firms' stock price fell further.[174] The firms chosen were Fannie Mae, Freddie Mac, and the primary dealers (large financial firms that conduct open market operations with the Federal Reserve).[175] Some market participants perceived this announcement as an explicit list of the firms that the government considered too big to fail. If this announcement was intended to rescue troubled firms, either by making short selling more difficult or by making too big to fail status more explicit, it did not work in all cases—in September 2008, Lehman Brothers entered bankruptcy, while Fannie Mae and Freddie Mac entered government conservatorship. Nor did the list closely correspond to which firms would or would not receive government assistance subsequently—American International Group (AIG) received assistance although it was not one of the 19 firms listed, while Lehman Brothers did not receive although it was included on the list.

The July ban was superseded by an SEC rule issued on September 18, 2008, that temporarily banned all short-selling of the stocks of 700 financial firms and an October 1, 2008, rule that imposed a permanent ban on naked short-selling.

Fannie Mae and Freddie Mac

Not only were Fannie Mae and Freddie Mac very large, their TBTF status was also influenced by their unusual status as government sponsored enterprises (GSEs). Because of unusual features such as their congressional charter, line of credit with the Treasury, dominance of the home mortgage secondary market, and original status as government agencies, investors perceived them as more likely to be backed by the government than other firms, although their securities had no explicit government guarantee. This perception allowed them to consistently borrow at a lower cost than other financial firms, despite holding relatively little capital. Before conservatorship, Fannie Mae and Freddie Mac were the only firms regulated by their federal regulator, whose independence and powers were limited compared to other regulators.[176] These institutional features led critics to argue that the GSEs enjoyed the benefits of "regulatory capture." Their regulator found them to meet the statutory definition of well capitalized as recently as July 2008.[177]

Holding mainly mortgage-backed securities and mortgages in their portfolios, they were uniquely vulnerable to the decline in the housing market and MBS prices. In July 2008, investor concern about persistent losses and the potential for future losses led to a sharp decline in stock prices and cast doubt on their ability to roll over maturing debt. Treasury Secretary Paulson argued that the solution to this problem was for Congress to grant him what he referred to as a "bazooka"—the

---

[174] Short selling consists of borrowing shares and selling them, in the hope that the short seller can buy back the borrowed shares at a lower price in the future. A short sale is "naked" if the seller does not actually borrow shares for delivery to the buyer. For more information, see CRS Report RS22099, *Regulation of Naked Short Selling*, by Mark Jickling.

[175] Kara Scannell and Tom Lauricella, "SEC Extends Short-Selling Rules," *Wall Street Journal*, July 30, 2008, p. C. 1.

[176] Limits on OFHEO's powers and independence are discussed in CRS Report RL32069, *Improving the Effectiveness of GSE Oversight: Legislative Proposals in the 108th Congress*, by Loretta Nott and Mark Jickling.

[177] Office of Federal Housing Enterprise Oversight, Statement of OFHEO Director James B. Lockhart, July 10, 2008.

authority for Treasury to provide the GSEs with unlimited funding. He argued that the bazooka would calm investor fears, and as a result would not need to be used. Congress provided this authority in the Housing and Economic Recovery Act (P.L. 110-289).

By September 2008, the government decided to take the GSEs into conservatorship following further losses.[178] Conservatorship means that the government has assumed the normal powers of the officers, board of directors, and shareholders, but the GSEs would continue business operations. In addition, the government would purchase their MBS and inject as much capital as needed to keep the firms solvent. In return, the government received warrants to purchase 79.9% of the companies' common stock, which would dilute existing shareholders when exercised. Management was also replaced and dividends on preferred shares were eliminated, but creditors, including subordinated debt holders, and counterparties suffered no losses.

One rationale for placing the GSEs in conservatorship was that their dominant role in mortgage-backed securities markets could not have been replaced quickly by the private sector given the housing downturn. Without them, mortgage credit would have become less available, placing further downward pressure on the housing market. Another rationale was the potential for contagion to counterparties and creditors given the large amount of GSE debt and GSE-guaranteed MBS outstanding.

To bridge the gap between the companies' assets and liabilities, the government provided $187.5 billion to the companies in exchange for preferred shares between 2008 and 2012. The government received $55 billion of dividends on those shares through 2012. Since then, the GSEs' assets have matched their liabilities and no further preferred share issuance has been needed. Under the existing agreement, the GSEs' profits (after dividend payments) would have accumulated in their coffers.[179] Treasury announced in August 2012 that, "(a)cting upon the commitment ... that the GSEs will be wound down and will not be allowed to retain profits, rebuild capital, and return to the market in their prior form," the preferred share agreements had been amended to replace the dividend and commitment fee with a "net income sweep" that would remit all profits to the Treasury.[180] Regardless of the amount remitted, the terms of the sweep do not allow for a reduction in the preferred shares outstanding. Thus, while Treasury has not recouped any principal, it earned a cumulative $202.8 billion in income through the first quarter of 2014—more than it outlayed.

In economic terms, the subsidy to the GSEs, which takes into account future losses and the opportunity cost inherent in the GSEs' ability to borrow at below market rates, was estimated by CBO to be $291 billion through 2009. Since this estimate was made in August 2009, the state of the housing market has improved considerably, which could reduce expected defaults and thus the size of the subsidy, were CBO to update its estimate. In addition, CBO assumes that the companies will continue to do business at below-market costs in the future that will lead to future subsidies from the government.[181]

---

[178] For more information, see CRS Report RL34661, *Fannie Mae's and Freddie Mac's Financial Problems*, by N. Eric Weiss.

[179] For more information, see Federal Housing Finance Agency, U.S. Treasury Support for Fannie Mae and Freddie Mac," Mortgage Market Note, no. 10-1, Jan. 20, 2010.

[180] U.S. Treasury, "Treasury Department Announces Further Steps to Expedite Wind Down of Fannie Mae and Freddie Mac," press release, August 16, 2012. The agreement allows the GSEs to build a capital reserve of $3 billion.

[181] Congressional Budget Office, *The Budgetary Cost of Fannie Mae and Freddie Mac*, Testimony before the (continued...)

Between December 2008 and March 2010, the Fed purchased $67 billion of debt issued by Freddie Mac and $67 billion issued by Fannie Mae as part of its "Large Scale Asset Purchases" (popularly known as quantitative easing). While the asset purchases were intended to provide support to mortgage markets and to stimulate overall economic conditions, another effect of these purchases was to reduce the GSEs' borrowing costs, all else equal. As these assets have matured, the Fed's holdings have declined over time. The Fed faces no default risk on its GSE holdings as long as the Treasury continues to stand behind the GSEs, and will not experience capital losses (or gains) as long as it continues to hold the securities to maturity. The Treasury and Fed have also purchased debt and MBS issued by the GSEs since 2008. The MBS purchases were made at market prices on the secondary market, so the purchases conferred no direct benefit to the GSEs, but had the effect of indirectly raising the price received by the GSEs for their MBS.

Lehman Brothers

Shortly after the failures of Fannie Mae and Freddie Mac, the investment bank Lehman Brothers experienced a liquidity crisis. Lehman Brothers was the 47th-largest firm by revenues in 2007 on *Fortune Magazine*'s Fortune 500 list.[182] Lehman Brothers was not a bank holding company regulated for safety and soundness, nor subject to the FDIC's resolution regime. Lehman Brothers was a unitary thrift holding company under OTS umbrella supervision; OTS was focused mainly on the health of the depository subsidiaries. It also complied with an SEC net capital rule.[183] Policy makers decided to allow Lehman Brothers to file for bankruptcy when it became clear that no other firm was willing to acquire the firm without government assistance. According to Bankruptcydata.com, Lehman Brothers was the largest firm by assets ever to file for bankruptcy.[184]

Lehman Brothers was larger than Bear Stearns and was involved in similar business lines. Bear Stearns had been saved with government assistance, and many market participants were surprised that a similar arrangement was not made for Lehman Brothers. Unlike Bear Stearns, Lehman Brothers had access to Fed lending facilities (created after the Bear Stearns crisis), but did not have enough collateral under the terms of the Fed program to borrow enough to meet its liquidity needs at the time of its failure. (This problem did not arise when the Fed rescued AIG the next day.) Policy makers argued that markets should not have expected government assistance because they had stressed since the Bear Stearns intervention that similar assistance could not be expected in the future and that failures were necessary to prevent moral hazard problems. Policy makers also argued that Lehman Brothers had plenty of time to defend themselves from the fate suffered by Bear Stearns by raising more capital and long-term liquidity. (Lehman Brothers did raise some in the summer of 2008.) Policy makers believed that they and counterparties were now well enough prepared for a counterparty failure that systemic risk could be contained.[185]

(...continued)

Committee on the Budget, U.S. House of Representatives, June 2011.

[182] List can be accessed at http://money.cnn.com/magazines/fortune/fortune500/2007/full_list/index.html.

[183] For more information, see CRS Report R43087, *Who Regulates Whom and How? An Overview of U.S. Financial Regulatory Policy for Banking and Securities Markets*, by Edward V. Murphy.

[184] http://www.bankruptcydata.com/Research/Largest_Overall_All-Time.pdf.

[185] For example, see Chairman Ben Bernanke, "Lessons from the Failure of Lehman Brothers," testimony before the Committee on Financial Services, U.S. House of Representatives, April 20, 2010, http://www.federalreserve.gov/newsevents/testimony/bernanke20100420a htm. Thomas Baxter, testimony before the Financial Crisis Inquiry Commission, September 1, 2010, http://fcic-static.law.stanford.edu/cdn_media/fcic-testimony/2010-0901-Baxter.pdf.

Some point to the complex, lengthy nature of Lehman Brothers' bankruptcy proceedings as evidence that Lehman Brothers was too big to fail, while others argue that bankruptcy proceedings have gone relatively smoothly and are successfully resolving the claims of creditors and counterparties in an orderly fashion.[186] A New York Fed study finds that creditors received an unusually low recovery rate from the Lehman bankruptcy.[187]

Where Lehman Brothers' failure proved more disruptive to financial markets was through its effects on money market mutual funds (MMF) and the commercial paper market. On September 16, 2008, a MMF called the Reserve Fund "broke the buck," meaning that the value of its shares had fallen below face value. This occurred because of losses it had taken on short-term debt issued by Lehman Brothers, which filed for bankruptcy on September 15, 2008. Money market investors had perceived "breaking the buck" to be highly unlikely, and its occurrence set off a run on money market funds, as investors simultaneously attempted to withdraw an estimated $250 billion of their investments—even from funds without exposure to Lehman Brothers.[188] MMFs are major investors in commercial paper, so this run greatly decreased the demand for new commercial paper.[189] Firms rely on the ability to issue new debt to roll over maturing debt to meet their liquidity needs. A blanket federal guarantee of MMFs and three Federal Reserve commercial paper programs were created to restore calm to these markets.[190]

Contagion from Lehman Brothers' failure also spread to its three remaining independent "bulge bracket" investment bank rivals, Merrill Lynch, Morgan Stanley, and Goldman Sachs. All three experienced liquidity strains following Lehman Brothers' failure, which all three survived, but only after fundamental changes to their business models. Merrill Lynch merged with Bank of America under financial strain, which would cause problems for Bank of America in the ensuing months. Goldman Sachs and Morgan Stanley changed their charters to become bank holding companies, under the umbrella supervision of the Federal Reserve. All three relied heavily on broadly based federal facilities to weather the storm. Borrowing from the Fed's Primary Dealer Credit Facility peaked at $48 billion for Morgan Stanley and $40 billion for Merrill Lynch on September 26, 2008, and at $17 billion for Goldman Sachs on October 10, 2008. All three firms also accessed the Fed's Term Securities Lending Facility throughout the fall and its Commercial Paper Funding Facility beginning in late October. Morgan Stanley and Goldman Sachs each received $10 billion in exchange for preferred shares through TARP's Capital Purchase Program on October 28, 2008, and $10 billion of CPP funds for Merrill Lynch were received by Bank of America after their merger.

---

[186] See CRS Report R40928, *Lehman Brothers and IndyMac: Comparing Resolution Regimes*, by David H. Carpenter.

[187] Michael Fleming and Asani Sarkar, "The Failure Resolution of Lehman Brothers," Federal Reserve Bank of New York, *Economic Policy Review*, vol. 20, no. 2, March 2014.

[188] Figure cited in Fed Chairman Ben Bernanke, "Financial Reform to Address Systemic Risk," speech at the Council on Foreign Relations, March 10, 2009, http://www.federalreserve.gov/newsevents/speech/bernanke20090310a.htm.

[189] There is debate over whether the money market run triggered by Lehman Brothers' bankruptcy should be considered to be caused by Lehman Brothers being TBTF. The view that attributes the run to TBTF interprets the run as triggered by concerns about the exposure of Lehman Brothers counterparties. The alternative view is that the run was triggered by concerns about holding paper issued by any financial firm with exposure to "toxic" MBS. Neither view is inconsistent with the fact that many of the funds that experienced runs were not holding paper issued by Lehman Brothers. See, for example, Daniel Tarullo, "Regulating Systemic Risk," speech at 2011 Credit Markets Symposium, Charlotte, North Carolina, March 31, 2011, http://www.federalreserve.gov/newsevents/speech/tarullo20110331a.htm.

[190] This section draws on information from CRS Report R41073, *Government Interventions in Response to Financial Turmoil*, by Baird Webel and Marc Labonte.

Although the Fed was not willing to rescue Lehman Brothers, it provided Lehman Brothers with liquidity for a short time to ease the bankruptcy process.[191] Lehman Brothers borrowed an average of $23 billion each day from the Fed's Primary Dealer Credit Facility, a broadly based emergency facility, from September 15, the day it filed for bankruptcy, to September 17, 2008.[192] Lehman Brothers also borrowed from the Fed's Term Securities Lending Facility frequently from March 2008 to September 12, 2008.

AIG

At the same time as the failure of Lehman Brothers, American International Group (AIG) ran into liquidity problems as a result of collateral calls on its credit default swaps and securities lending program.[193]

AIG is a large financial firm operating domestically and abroad; at the time of the crisis, its insurance operations were the fifth largest in the world. While AIG is often thought of as an insurance company, it was a complex financial institution with many different types of subsidiaries, such as AIG Financial Products, which Fed Chairman Bernanke reportedly likened to a hedge fund.[194] Its overall legal structure was a unitary thrift regulated by the Office of Thrift Supervision (OTS), although its thrift operations were relatively small. AIG's insurance subsidiaries were regulated at the state level. Losses were centered in the Financial Products subsidiary and its securities lending program; as its umbrella regulator, OTS was focused mainly on the health of the depository subsidiaries. OTS has testified that it did not fully foresee the potential losses that transactions undertaken by AIG Financial Products posed to the holding company.[195]

Unlike Lehman Brothers, policy makers decided that the systemic risk implications of an AIG failure were too great. AIG was listed as the 10th-largest firm by revenues in 2007 on *Fortune Magazine*'s Fortune 500 list.[196] On September 16, 2008, the Fed announced that it was taking action to support AIG. Using emergency authority, this support took the form of a secured two-year line of credit with a value of up to $85 billion and a high interest rate (set at 8.5 percentage points above the London Interbank Offered Rate). Although the Fed denied assistance to Lehman Brothers on the grounds that it lacked acceptable collateral, the loan to AIG was collateralized by the general assets of AIG.[197] In addition, the government received warrants to purchase up to 79.9% of the equity in AIG.

Once the determination to assist AIG had been made, assistance arguably became open-ended, and more government assistance was provided on several subsequent occasions. On October 8,

---

[191] Thomas Baxter, testimony before the Financial Crisis Inquiry Commission, September 1, 2010, http://fcic-static.law.stanford.edu/cdn_media/fcic-testimony/2010-0901-Baxter.pdf.

[192] Data from http://www.federalreserve.gov/newsevents/reform_pdcf.htm.

[193] See CRS Report R40438, *Federal Government Assistance for American International Group (AIG)*, by Baird Webel

[194] Craig Torres and Hugh Son, "Bernanke Says Insurer AIG Operated Like a Hedge Fund," *Bloomberg*, March 3, 2009.

[195] Scott Polakoff, Testimony before the Subcommittee on Capital Markets, Insurance, and Government Sponsored Enterprises, House Committee on Financial Services, U.S. House of Representatives, March 18, 2009, http://www.house.gov/apps/list/hearing/financialsvcs_dem/ots_3.18.09.pdf.

[196] List can be accessed at http://money.cnn.com/magazines/fortune/fortune500/2007/full_list/index.html.

[197] Chairman Ben Bernanke, Testimony Before the House Committee on Financial Services, March 24, 2009.

2008, the Fed announced that it would lend AIG up to an additional $37.8 billion against securities held by its insurance subsidiaries. These securities had been previously lent out and were not available as collateral at the time of the original intervention, increasing AIG's cash flow problems. In October 2008, AIG also announced that it had applied to the Fed's general Commercial Paper Facility and was approved to borrow up to $20.9 billion at the facility's standard terms.

The financial support for AIG was restructured in early November 2008. The restructured financial support included up to a $60 billion loan from the Fed, with the term lengthened to five years and the interest rate reduced by 5.5 percentage points; $40 billion in preferred share purchases through the TARP through a new program created for AIG called the "Systemically Significant Failing Institutions Program"; up to $52.5 billion total in asset purchases by the Fed through two Limited Liability Corporations (LLCs) known as Maiden Lane II and Maiden Lane III. AIG contributed an additional $6 billion for the LLCs and will bear the first $6 billion in any losses on the asset values. By 2012, the Maiden Lanes had received more from asset sales than the Fed had contributed to their purchases. Principal and interest were recouped, and further gains from these LLCs were shared between the Fed and AIG.

The 79.9% common equity position of the government in AIG remained essentially unchanged after the restructuring of the intervention, although assistance was increased. Additional restructurings were announced in March 2010 and September 2010. In the latter restructuring, the Federal Reserve loan was repaid in full and the preferred shares were converted into common equity. This increases the risk and potential reward for the government from its AIG holdings since the common equity can rise or fall in value based on market conditions and the future financial performance of AIG. Warrants initially valued at $1.2 billion were also issued to AIG's private shareholders at this time, transferring value from the government to shareholders. The government sold its common equity stake between May 2011 and December 2012.

With each restructuring, costs were reduced for AIG and risks were shifted away from AIG to the government. Policy makers initially provided loans with very high interest rates out of moral hazard concerns, but found that punitive conditions decreased the ongoing viability of the company (and, hence, the probability that the assistance would be repaid). Therefore, when assistance was revised, conditions typically became less punitive. Since the government held 92.6% of the common stock in AIG at the peak, however, a case can be made that the benefits of any restructuring that improves AIG's future profitability mostly accrues to the government.

On a cash-flow basis, the Fed and Treasury combined ultimately received $23 billion more than they outlayed to AIG. Whether this resulted in an economic profit for the federal government or a subsidy to AIG depends on the opportunity cost of those funds, based on the risks that the government undertook and the time value of money. CBO has made such a calculation, and estimates that the TARP portion of the assistance to AIG will have a net cost of $15 billion over the lifetime of the assistance.[198] At the time of the Fed's intervention, CBO estimated a $2 billion subsidy for the Fed portion of the assistance; since the Fed's intervention turned out to be cash-flow positive and CBO has revised downward its estimates of TARP subsidies over time, that amount could be re-estimated downward if CBO were to update it.

---

[198] Congressional Budget Office, *Report on the Troubled Asset Relief Program*, April 2014, Table 3.

Washington Mutual and Wachovia

Two large banks, Washington Mutual and Wachovia, were successfully resolved by the FDIC through mergers during the 2008 crisis, at no cost to the taxpayers.

Washington Mutual was a thrift holding company. Its depository subsidiary experienced depositor runs in 2008 following losses. It was the 81st-largest firm by revenues in 2007 on *Fortune Magazine*'s Fortune 500 list and the largest thrift holding company.[199] Depositors withdrew $9.4 billion between July 12 and July 30, and $15 billion between September 11 and 26—the closest the 2008 crisis saw to a traditional bank run.[200] On September 25, the thrift was taken into receivership by the FDIC. It was resolved through a purchase and assumption agreement with J.P. Morgan Chase. As part of the agreement, J.P. Morgan Chase paid $1.9 billion to assume the claims of uninsured depositors, counterparties with qualified financial contracts, and secured creditors; it did not assume the claims of unsecured creditors or equity holders.[201] The remainder of the company filed for bankruptcy on September 26. Thus, the receivership required no federal funds, and the moral hazard problem was mitigated since unsecured creditors and equity holders suffered losses. J.P. Morgan Chase's willingness to pay to assume other liabilities implies that it believed the remaining assets were sufficient to honor those liabilities.

Washington Mutual received a $1 billion, 28-day loan from the Federal Reserve's Term Auction Facility on September 11, 2008. The bank was closed by the FDIC on September 25, 2008, and the loan was repaid after its merger. Since the loan was fully collateralized and the Fed receives priority ahead of other creditors, it appears to have posed little risk to the taxpayers in the face of receivership. Nonetheless, the loan appears to have been a departure from Fed policy since the Fed's broadly based lending programs were intended to provide liquidity to solvent firms.

Washington Mutual could be seen as an example of a TBTF bank that experienced an orderly resolution through the FDIC's resolution regime at no cost to the taxpayers. Or it could be seen as too small to be relevant to the TBTF debate.

Wachovia (the 46th-largest firm on *Fortune Magazine*'s Fortune 500 list in 2007) faced runs soon after Washington Mutual failed. According to Federal Reserve testimony,

> The day after the failure of WaMu, Wachovia Bank depositors accelerated the withdrawal of significant amounts from their accounts. In addition, wholesale funds providers withdrew liquidity support from Wachovia. It appeared likely that Wachovia would soon become unable to fund its operations.[202]

---

[199] List can be accessed at http://money.cnn.com/magazines/fortune/fortune500/2007/full_list/index html. Scott G. Alvarez, "The Acquisition of Wachovia Corporation by Wells Fargo & Company," Testimony Before the Financial Crisis Inquiry Commission, Washington, D.C., September 1, 2010.

[200] Kirsten Grind, "WaMu's Final Days," *Puget Sound Business Journal*, Friday, September 25, 2009, http://seattle.bizjournals.com/seattle/stories/2009/09/28/story1.html?page=1.

[201] Federal Deposit Insurance Corporation, "JPMorgan Chase Acquires Banking Operations of Washington Mutual," Press Release PR-85-2008, September 25, 2008.

[202] Scott G. Alvarez, "The Acquisition of Wachovia Corporation by Wells Fargo & Company," Testimony Before the Financial Crisis Inquiry Commission, Washington, D.C., September 1, 2010, http://www.federalreserve.gov/newsevents/testimony/alvarez20100901a htm.

According to the Fed, problems at Wachovia were unforeseen, making the bank both a victim and a potential transmitter of contagion:

> At the time, Wachovia was considered "well capitalized" by regulatory standards and until very recently had not generally been thought to be in danger of failure, so there were fears that the failure of Wachovia would lead investors to doubt the financial strength of other organizations in similar situations, making it harder for those institutions to raise capital and other funding.[203]

On September 27 and 28, Wells Fargo and Citigroup placed competing bids to acquire Wachovia. Initially, those bids were contingent on federal assistance. FDIC assistance under the systemic risk exception to least cost resolution had been approved.[204] Later, Wells Fargo revised its offer, acquiring Wachovia without federal assistance and averting a receivership.

Neither the Washington Mutual nor the Wachovia acquisitions were found to breach the Riegle-Neal 10% nationwide deposit cap. JP Morgan Chase's acquisition of Washington Mutual's deposits and other assets occurred through an FDIC purchase and assumption arrangement. The 10% deposit cap does not apply to an FDIC purchase and assumption. In its approval of Wells Fargo's acquisition of Wachovia, the Fed noted that using the most current data, the merged entity would be above the 10% deposit limit. The Fed then argued that since that data were released with a lag, projections of *current* deposit data indicated that the merger would probably fall below the 10% cap.[205]

Although the Fed's Term Auction Facility was intended for healthy firms, Wachovia received nine Term Auction Facility loans between September 11, 2008, and February 26, 2009, including $5 billion on September 25, 2008, one day before the run on Wachovia began. Its merger with Wells Fargo was announced on October 3, 2008.

TARP, Citigroup, Bank of America, and the Stress Tests

The first and largest program initiated under the Troubled Asset Relief Program (TARP) was the Capital Purchase Program (CPP).[206] The purpose of the CPP was to provide banks and bank holding companies (BHC) with preferred shares to increase their capital buffers against future losses at a time when it was difficult for banks to access private capital. The CPP was intended for healthy banks of all sizes and unsuitable candidates were rejected. Therefore, it does not closely match the definition of bailout used in this report, which implies assistance to unhealthy firms, or TBTF assistance. Nevertheless, CPP funds went to banks that later failed (14 mostly small banks, as of December 2011)[207] and the first recipients were the nine largest BHCs, all of whom had fully repaid CPP shares by 2010. If limited to healthy banks and purchased at market rates, preferred shares impose limited risk on taxpayers. Despite the handful of losses on CPP

---

[203] *Ibid.*

[204] *Ibid.*

[205] Federal Reserve, "Statement by the Board of Governors of the Federal Reserve System Regarding the Application and Notices by Wells Fargo and Company to Acquire Wachovia Corporation," October 12, 2008, p. 7, http://www.federalreserve.gov/newsevents/press/orders/orders20081021a1.pdf.

[206] For more information on all TARP programs, see CRS Report R41427, *Troubled Asset Relief Program (TARP): Implementation and Status*, by Baird Webel.

[207] U.S. Department of Treasury, *TARP Monthly 105(a) Report – December 2011*, January 2012. The largest failure was CIT Group, with $76 billion in consolidated assets in the first quarter of 2009.

investments in small banks, CBO has estimated that the government will ultimately earn an overall economic profit (i.e., earn an above market rate of return) from the CPP from dividends and warrants. In October 2012, CBO estimated that profit to be $18 billion.[208]

After the initial disbursement of CPP funds, Citigroup and Bank of America received additional TARP capital injections and asset guarantees for their balance sheet holdings through a special TARP program with no other recipients. The additional capital paid a higher dividend rate than the CPP shares. Other TARP programs included programs to assist AIG (discussed above) and the automakers. As will be discussed, the program for automakers was used to provide special assistance to two financial firms, Chrysler Financial and GMAC (later renamed Ally Financial).

Following the additional TARP capital injections, Citigroup remained well capitalized according to regulatory standards.[209] It appears that without TARP funds Citigroup would have fallen to slightly below the Fed's minimum Tier 1 Leverage requirements of 4% at the end of 2008, assuming they had not raised private capital in the absence of TARP funds.[210] Regulations require BHCs to submit a plan to the Fed in a timely manner if they fall below minimum capital requirements.[211] In February 2009, Citigroup and the federal government reached an agreement to convert up to $27.5 billion of Citigroup's TARP preferred shares into common equity. This agreement had the result of boosting Citigroup's common equity ratios and ending dividend payments to the government.[212] It also exposed the government to greater risk and potentially greater return on its investments, since common equity can rise and fall in value, unlike the TARP preferred shares. Citigroup was the largest financial firm in the country and eighth-largest firm overall on *Fortune Magazine*'s 2007 Fortune 500 list.[213]

Bank of America's financial problems centered mainly on its acquisitions of Countrywide and another very large financial firm, the investment bank Merrill Lynch. At the time of the Lehman Brothers crisis, Merrill Lynch also came under financial pressure as a result of its similar business model, forcing it to seek a merger partner. Merrill Lynch (the 22nd-largest firm on *Fortune Magazine*'s Fortune 500 list in 2007) was larger than either of those firms. In September 2008, Bank of America and Merrill Lynch reached an agreement in principle to merge. As financial conditions deteriorated further, Bank of America considered pulling out of the merger. To prevent this, according to the Treasury Secretary at the time, the government agreed to purchase another $20 billion of preferred shares through TARP and enter into a federal asset guarantee agreement.[214] The merger was finalized in January 2009, and Bank of America received the

---

[208] Congressional Budget Office, *Report on the Troubled Asset Relief Program*, October 2012.

[209] In their regulatory call reports, banks report capital ratios for three measures: Total Risk-Based Capital, Tier 1 Risk-Based Capital, and Tier 1 Leverage. For large BHCs, the Fed sets a minimum Tier 1 leverage requirement of 3% of total assets for banks receiving the highest regulatory rating and 4% of total assets for all other firms (12 CFR 225 Appendix D). The regulatory rating that firms receive is confidential. For Tier 1 Risk-Based Capital and Total Risk-Based Capital, respectively, the Fed sets minimum requirements of 4% and 8% of risk-weighted assets.

[210] At the holding company level, Citigroup reported $118.8 billion of Tier 1 Capital in its December 2008 call report; of this total, $45 billion was from TARP. An estimate for the other two regulatory capital ratio measures cannot be easily calculated.

[211] 12 CFR Part 225, Subpart J.

[212] Citigroup, "Citi to Exchange Preferred Securities for Common, Increasing Tangible Common Equity to as Much as $81 Billion," press release, February 27, 2009, http://www.citigroup.com/citi/press/2009/090227a htm.

[213] List can be accessed at http://money.cnn.com/magazines/fortune/fortune500/2007/full_list/index.html.

[214] Henry Paulson, Testimony before the Committee on Oversight and Government Reform, U.S. House of Representatives, July 16, 2009, posted at http://online.wsj.com/public/resources/documents/WSJ-20090715-PaulsonTestimony.pdf.

---

additional TARP shares shortly thereafter; the asset guarantee was never finalized. In its March 2009 call report, Bank of America remained well capitalized according to regulatory standards.[215] It appears that even without TARP funds Bank of America would have remained above the Fed's minimum Tier 1 leverage requirements of 4% in that quarter.[216]

In May 2009, the Federal Reserve released the results of the Supervisory Capital Assessment Program, its "stress tests" for the 19 largest bank holding companies.[217] The stress tests were meant to determine whether these banks would remain well capitalized in the event of a downside economic scenario. The tests required banks to be able to maintain Tier 1 Risk-Based Capital of 6% and Tier 1 Common Capital of 4% in this scenario. Of the participants, 10 of 19 were found to be well capitalized against future losses; of those 10, the 9 participating in TARP bought back their preferred shares and exited the program shortly thereafter. Of the other nine that required additional capital to withstand hypothetical losses under the adverse scenario, seven (including Bank of America, which was required to raised $33.9 billion) were able to raise the needed capital without government funds; GMAC required TARP funds (through the Automotive Industry Financing Program) to raise the needed capital; and Citigroup, which was required to raise $5.5 billion, met the threshold for Tier 1 Common Capital in part by converting more of its existing CPP preferred shares into common shares. After the preferred shares were converted to common equity, the government owned about one-third of the company.[218]

In December 2009, Citigroup bought back $20 billion of TARP preferred securities outstanding, replacing those shares with private capital, and terminated the government's asset guarantee for a fee. In March 2010, the Treasury announced plans to dispose of its common shares in Citigroup by the end of the year. The government ultimately sold these shares for $31.9 billion, or $6.9 billion more than the initial assistance extended. Treasury reports that for the three programs assisting Citigroup combined, it had a positive cash flow of $13.4 billion.[219]

In December 2009, Bank of America repurchased all of its TARP preferred shares, replacing those shares with private capital, and paid a fee to cancel the asset guarantee that was negotiated but never entered into.

The experience with Bank of America and Citigroup is quite different from the experience with AIG and the GSEs. While TARP funds kept Bank of America's and Citigroup's capital levels above the minimally required level, neither firm is believed to have been close to insolvency—

---

[215] The first quarter of 2009 was the first call report to incorporate TARP shares and the Merrill Lynch merger. In their regulatory call reports, banks report capital ratios for three measures: Total Risk-Based Capital, Tier 1 Risk-Based Capital, and Tier 1 Leverage. For large BHCs, the Fed sets a minimum Tier 1 leverage requirement of 3% of total assets for banks receiving the highest regulatory rating and 4% of total assets for all other firms (12 CFR 225 Appendix D). The regulatory rating that firms receive is confidential. For Tier 1 Risk-Based Capital and Total Risk-Based Capital, respectively, the Fed sets minimum requirements of 4% and 8% of risk-weighted assets.

[216] At the holding company level, Bank of America reported $117.9 billion of Tier 1 Capital in its December 2008 call report; of this total, $45 billion was from TARP. An estimate for the other two capital ratio measures cannot easily be calculated.

[217] Federal Reserve, *The Supervisory Capital Assessment Program: Overview of Results*, May 7, 2009. For an evaluation, see Special Inspector General for Troubled Asset Relief Program, *Exiting TARP: Repayments by the Largest Financial Institutions*, SIGTARP report 11-005, September 29, 2011.

[218] Citigroup, *Supervisory Capital Assessment Program Results – Update on Exchange Offer*, May 7, 2009, http://www.citigroup.com/citi/fin/data/p090507a.pdf.

[219] U.S. Treasury, "Treasury Prices Sale of Citigroup Subordinated Notes for Proceeds of $894 Million," press release, February 5, 2013.

although it is unknown what would have happened to Merrill Lynch had Bank of America not acquired it. Bank of America repaid TARP funds in full in December 2009, and the government fully divested from Citigroup in 2010. CBO has estimated that the government earned an economic profit, calculated using a risk-adjusted discount rate, of $8 billion from its special assistance to the two companies.[220]

GMAC

While Congress authorized TARP to "purchase, and to make and fund commitments to purchase, troubled assets from any financial institution, on such terms and conditions as are determined by the Secretary, and in accordance with this Act and the policies and procedures developed and published by the Secretary," TARP funding was also used to facilitate the bankruptcy process for GM and Chrysler.[221] Economists have generally focused on financial firms as being TBTF because of the interconnectedness inherent in financial intermediation; determining whether automakers can be TBTF is beyond the scope of this report.

In conjunction with the automakers, two financial firms related to the automakers, GMAC and Chrysler Financial, also received TARP assistance. Chrysler Financial was a relatively small financial firm, and it repaid its $1.5 billion TARP loan in full with interest by July 2009. GMAC received several rounds of TARP funding in order to return its capital levels to acceptable levels. After converting to a bank holding company during the crisis, GMAC was the 10th-largest bank holding company, with $180 billion in assets, in the first quarter of 2009. It dominated dealer floorplan financing for GM and Chrysler, and reportedly had three times the market share of its five largest competitors in auto financing.[222]

TARP first purchased $5 billion of GMAC preferred shares in December 2008 and lent $884 million to GM, which was later transferred to GMAC, as part of the initial assistance provided to the automakers. As discussed above, GMAC was one of the nine bank holding companies that were required to raise additional capital under the May 2009 stress tests. It was the only one of those nine that raised the capital through additional TARP disbursements, rather than through private markets. The government purchased an additional $7.5 billion of preferred shares and converted the $884 million loan into 35.4% of GMAC's common equity in May 2009. The government then purchased $2.54 billion of trust preferred securities and an additional $1.25 billion of preferred shares in December 2009. At the same time, it converted $3 billion in preferred shares for 20.9% of GMAC's common equity. In December 2010, it converted an additional $5.5 billion of preferred shares into 17.5% of GMAC's common equity; $5.9 billion of preferred shares remain outstanding, and the government has sold the trust preferred securities to private investors at face value. This made recoupment of funds for the government dependent on the future value of GMAC (renamed Ally Financial).[223] To date, the government has sold its preferred shares back to GMAC and some of its common stock to private investors. Although the government still holds shares, the proceeds from share sales plus income received less writeoffs to date has slightly exceeded its total initial outlays. CBO does not estimate a separate subsidy

---

[220] Congressional Budget Office, *Report on the Troubled Asset Relief Program*, April 2014.

[221] More information can be found in out-of-print CRS Report R40003, *U.S. Motor Vehicle Industry: Federal Financial Assistance and Restructuring*, coordinated by Bill Canis, available upon request.

[222] Congressional Oversight Panel, *January Oversight Report*, January 13, 2011, p. 82.

[223] CRS Report R41846, *Government Assistance for GMAC/Ally Financial: Unwinding the Government Stake*, by Baird Webel and Bill Canis.

cost for the government's assistance to GMAC, but estimates "a small net cost" for assistance to GMAC and Chrysler Financial combined.[224]

Author Contact Information

Marc Labonte
Specialist in Macroeconomic Policy
mlabonte@crs.loc.gov, 7-0640

Acknowledgments

The author would like to thank Darryl Getter, Mark Jickling, Edward Murphy, Maureen Murphy, Baird Webel, and Eric Weiss for helpful comments and assistance.

---

[224] Congressional Budget Office, *Report on the Troubled Asset Relief Program*, April 2014, p. 6.